U. S. MAIL

The Story of the United States Postal Service

U. S. MAIL

The Story of the United States Postal Service

by
ARTHUR E. Ellsworth SUMMERFIELD
as told to
Charles Hurd

HOLT, RINEHART AND WINSTON
New York

First Edition

Library of Congress Catalog Card Number: 60-10747

88225–0110

Printed in the United States of America

TABLE OF CONTENTS

Part I

Part II

Part III

DEDICATED

To my lovely wife, Miriam, a source of inspiration and strength, a devoted mother to our fine children. Her love, respect, and admiration I shall always cherish.

To my colleagues who brought to the Post Office Department urgently needed abilities in many vital areas. Their personal sacrifices made possible the creation of a team of men with broad experience, great imagination, and administrative know-how to manage the affairs of the Government's greatest peace-time operation.

To the 550,000 postal employees for their loyal support and their dedicated efforts.

To those members of the Congress whose imagination, integrity, and dedication enabled the Post Office Department to initiate its programs of modernization and mechanization.

To my colleagues in the President's Cabinet for their friendship, support, and co-operation.

To the men and women in business and industry who gave so freely of their counsel and advice.

And to President Dwight D. Eisenhower for his inspiring leadership, wisdom, and unfailing support. Under his personal sponsorship many important legislative enactments were executed enabling the Post Office Department to provide better, more efficient mail service.

Arthur E. Summerfield
Postmaster General

PART I

PART I

1

The Biggest Business
in the World

In December of 1952, President-elect Eisenhower invited me to serve in his Cabinet as Postmaster General of the United States. I was surprised and pleased—but neither my surprise nor pleasure matched the amazement with which I looked around in the days after I took office the following January 20.

I knew that the postal operations were huge, that I was assuming management of what amounted to the biggest business in the world.

There was reason for me to feel a special loyalty to the postal service, at least from the viewpoint of the men and women directly serving its patrons.

U.S. MAIL

My father, William Henry Summerfield, had been appointed a rural letter carrier in 1898, one year before I was born. He served in the environs of our home town of Pinconning, Michigan. For a number of years my family lived next door to the Pinconning Post Office. During that time Mr. George Barie, an uncle of my mother, Cora Edith Summerfield, was Postmaster.

I came to know early in life the genuine meaning of the old saying, "The mail must go through," as I watched the dedicated postal employees of those more primitive days push their way on foot through knee-deep snow when most people were staying close to their hearths inside.

But as a citizen generally, I had given little thought to the mail system which served me. I dropped my letters in the box and gave them no further thought, taking it for granted they would arrive at their destination in a reasonable time. There was no real hint of the tremendous complexities or the many very serious problems involved in the operations that moved those letters.

My first shock came on my second day in office when I asked for an operating statement of the business. I was told that no statement for the preceding month would be available for seventeen months! To a man with a background in business, where current operating statements are a first essential to sound management, this was incredible. To my further amazement, I discovered that the Post Office Department employed not a single certified public accountant—and here was a business with cash transactions totaling 20 billion dollars a year.

A few days later, I began an inspection trip to major post offices, in the course of which I saw employees struggling to handle tremendous volumes and bulks of mail with virtually no modern material-handling equipment. In New York City, the largest and busiest postal center in the world, the mail flowing into the Grand Central post office literally had to go through a three-foot-wide door. In Denver, employees were sorting mail under a canopy on the sidewalk during a snowstorm. There was not sufficient space inside the cluttered buildings to process all the volume of mail.

Almost everywhere work was being done with shopworn equipment in run-down, overcrowded, poorly lighted postal buildings constructed years before. Most tasks were being done by hand, too slowly and too expensively, in the same way they had been done in the days of the first Postmaster General—Benjamin Franklin.

It was appalling to consider the total effect of this plight in post offices throughout the country, handling mail in 1953 at the rate of 49 *billion* letters and 1 billion parcels a year.

Pay scales for the 524,000 postal employees bore little relation to the realities of ability and responsibility. In many post offices, janitors were being paid more than were the postmasters. There was no program of training or recruitment.

The organizational structure could only be described as primitive. Some 40,000 postmasters were reporting directly to Washington for instruction on even the most trivial matters.

At the headquarters in Washington, there was no research and development department; no mechanization study or work in progress; no department of personnel to direct, help, and train the more than 500,000 postal employees. There was no plan for developing efficiencies capable of meeting even partially the tremendous new burdens and costs which were mounting with our national population expansion and public demands for modern service.

Finally, and most disturbing of all, there came the revelation that the postal service was being subsidized by the United States Treasury at a rate of 2 million dollars a day.

Like most other Americans, I had always thought that when

11

anyone paid the postage on a letter, magazine or circular, he was paying roughly the cost of handling it. But such was far from the case, and the cost to the Government of making up the difference was growing by large leaps every year.

These were the reasons, then, why President Eisenhower specifically charged me to restore postal efficiency, revitalize postal morale, and operate the Department on a break-even basis.

If the full significance of this directive came as something of a surprise to me, it was because the postal problems had been the best-kept secret in government. The Hoover Commission had made a very able and comprehensive evaluation of the Post Office Department and recommended some basic changes in its procedures. This report, which was to become a valuable guidepost in our program to modernize the postal establishment, was resting snugly in the files.

The situation I am describing was not the fault of any one individual or any administration. It was the result of cumulative periods of neglect and of "make-do" during the war years when all our emphasis understandably was placed on the urgencies of national defense. But in 1953 the great American postal establishment was creaky from neglect, ruinously ridden with deficits, and archaic in operation. It was approaching a point where a serious breakdown was imminent. No government agency ever was in more urgent need of overhauling and revitalization.

I hope that the foregoing will not in any way give the impression that I have ever had anything but respect for the great traditions and services of the American postal establishment. To recognize critical problems that need solving is not to deny pride or to question basic values.

Our postal service is an indispensable part of the life of virtually every citizen. To people in every city and village and itself depends on the morale and integrity of the rank-and-file employees—qualities reflected in the famous inscription chiseled in stone on the façade of the New York City Post Office:

> Neither snow, nor rain, nor heat, nor gloom of night stays these couriers from the swift completion of their appointed rounds.

Who are these couriers? What is their tradition?

It is one of faithfulness and loyalty. Instance: Postmaster Beardsley of North Lansing, New York, appointed by John Quincy Adams, served under twenty Presidents of the United States, and remained at his post for seventy-five years.

It is one of firmness and integrity of administration. Instance: The following letter written by a postmaster:

> Mr. Spears:
> At your request, I send you a receipt for the postage on your paper. I am somewhat surprised at your request. I will, however, comply with it. The law requires newspaper postage to be paid in advance, and now that I have waited a full year, you choose to wound my feelings by insinuating that unless you get a receipt, I will probably make you pay again.
>
> Respectfully signed,
> Abraham Lincoln
> Postmaster
> Salem, Illinois.

It is one of honesty. Instance: Postmaster Workman of Bald Knob, West Virginia, was raided by Confederate soldiers while doing his job in 1862. After holding him prisoner for twenty-four hours, the soldiers departed, taking $16.06 worth of stamps. The office was subsequently closed. When Postmaster Workman was able to reopen it after the Civil War, he reviewed his accounts and deducted $16.06 from his first pay check to make up the value of the stamps he had "lost."

15

It is one of dependability. Instance: When the Hope Diamond, presumably the most valuable stone in the United States, was sent from New York to Washington, it traveled by regular registered first-class mail, handled by many postal employees as "routine."

It is one of reliability. Instance: In the entire seven years of my own experience as Postmaster General, among almost 40,000 postmasters, working with one of the world's finest inspection services, less than 300 have been removed for cause, including simple inefficiency or inability to handle their jobs.

Beyond the innumerable instances of special loyalties that can be cited are the daily routines of the rural route men and women who carry word of emergency or illness, give warning of disaster, and perform countless services—traditions dating from a period when they were the only available daily messengers.

Postal employees in every part of the service hold in deep respect all these traditions, many of which were born in the years that saw the birth of our nation itself.

With pride we date the establishment of the United States postal service from July 26, 1775, when it was authorized by the Continental Congress, with Franklin as our first Postmaster General. Actually, postal service in this country, dating from 1639 under the British Crown, is almost as old as any in the modern world. Franklin was no politically appointed novice when this trust was handed to him, for he had been the Colonial Postmaster General for the British Colonies in North America from 1735 until 1774, when he was dismissed because of his sympathy with the cause of the American revolutionists. What sympathy that was and how great its significance!

It was Franklin who, by enforcement of the sanctity of the

mails, enabled the Committees of Correspondence—John Hancock, Samuel Adams, and John Adams in Massachusetts; Thomas Jefferson, James Madison, and Patrick Henry in Virginia, among others—to concert the plans that eventually led to the meeting in Philadelphia at which the Declaration of Independence was written.

In less than two hundred years have come the massive developments in communications that have made correspondence by all individuals a commonplace, instead of a great luxury. In 1800 it cost six cents to send a single-sheet letter sixty miles (two sheets cost twelve cents, etc.) at a time when Delmonico's fashionable restaurant in New York served a full-course dinner for twelve cents. One letter sent between family members might cost a day's wages for a workman. And letters of emergency import received by poor families might render a serious financial blow, because they were sent *collect*. The postage stamp for prepayment of mail was still far in the future.

Mail service was still a luxury long after our changing social patterns had begun to recognize man's essential right to freedom of speech, religion, and thought, and the need for equal justice for all. The roots of this service, before our own beginnings, lay at the level of high privilege for the governing classes—the powerful, the rich, and the aristocracy—not for the governed.

The very traditions that have given the development of communcations a glamorous history spanning twenty-five hundred years too often gloss over the fact that the revolution in concept of mail, as developed in our country, has been as important, or more important, than the mechanical methods of delivering it.

Daniel Webster declaimed in 1823: "Mind is the great lever of all things." He was speaking of the power of ideas that already had won freedom for the United States and were laying the groundwork for its future development. But the ideas would have had no distribution without written communication. In fact, before Webster reached the end of his life, the postal service had become cheaper and truly national, and special services had been established for the free distribution of county newspapers and the cheap distribution of books.

As in so many cases of human development, the first use of the postal idea was as another weapon to perpetuate control over masses of persons by those in power. It was first an extension of privilege and later, as in much of our world today, a means of censorship or spying through clandestine controls.

The first recorded organized postal service was established twenty-five hundred years ago by King Cyrus the Great of Persia. His royal messengers, operating on scheduled routes over "post roads," with their progress impeded at the pain of death, carried royal edicts and reports of governors from one end of the Persian Empire to the other. Little about the mail service had changed five hundred years later when it was the tool of the Roman Emperors. Julius Caesar had a courier service that carried imperial reports from London to Rome or contrariwise in twenty-six days. But here again the service existed to serve despotic control, not to broaden the life of the people of the Empire. So such services remained for yet another fifteen hundred years, except for a period of apparently utter extinction in the Dark Ages.

Then in 1464, as a part of the great broadening of men's capabilities that came with the Renaissance, King Louis XI of France established the first "modern" postal service to help unify control over the country after five centuries of civil wars and intrigues. Messengers who announced their arrival by blowing on golden horns, whose lives and schedules were protected by the death penalty exacted of anyone interfering with them, were given the complete privilege of *Couriers du Roi.* In succeeding reigns the privilege of using the royal mails was extended to other members of royalty, to the aristocracy, then to wealthy businessmen, and finally to all—at about the time that postal service, whose beginnings will be described later, reached the American Colonies.

Henry VIII established the first postal service in England, again as the exclusive prerogative of the crown—adopting the name "post" from its French equivalent. Remount stations for carriers were called "posting" stations, and the attendants "postillions." Hence the mounted messenger service was a "post" service, and later became known as the "postal service." The old post stations soon developed inns for riders and stables for horses. Eventually there were larger buildings to accommodate travelers and their horses and carriages. These marked the beginnings of most of the famous old inns or hotels in today's world. No one traveled for pleasure three centuries ago.

The Elizabethan service developed within a century into one available, even though at excessive cost, to anyone who could pay the charges. And there began the idea of the sanctity of the mail—not yet implying freedom from censors or spying eyes, but making responsibility for delivery paramount to any avoidable or capricious delay. Many of the old English letters, written on heavy parchment, folded, and sealed with wax, had written on them: "Haste, Post, Haste, for Thye Lyfe, for Thye Lyfe, Haste." From which comes our common modern word "posthaste."

And by the time the British mail had become a public service of a sort, the beginnings of such a service had come to the colonies—a route from Boston to New York, under private contract but sacred in its mission. Which is why the original route of America's oldest highway—U.S. No. 1—connecting these cities by erratic twists along the ragged New England coast, is still known familiarly as the Boston Post Road.

For the sake of perspective, it may be pointed out that our modern postal history—spanning less than two hundred years of our existence as a nation—even so began in an era when railroads, motorized water and highway transport, and airplanes were yet to be conceived. Each, like the jet airplane and the guided missile, had to go through a pioneering stage as part of the program for communication of the written word.

2

Today's Postal Service
Challenge

Have you counted your mail at any time? Added up the letters you write and the advertisements and periodicals sent to you?

If these average one a day, you are an average user of the mails. We know that some persons with wide correspondence and those in larger communities who are flooded with mail other than letters will laugh at this as being ridiculously low. But it is statistically correct.

The United States mail reaches a volume equivalent to two thirds of all the world's mail on the basis of handling slightly more than 350 pieces a year for each member of its population, including newborn infants. This means that our postal service in 1960, serving about 180 million persons, must collect, transport, sort, and deliver into the mailbox or hand of the recipient more than 63 billion pieces of mail, plus 1 billion parcels, almost one fourth more than the 1953 volume.

Just prior to the turn of the century, in 1890, mail volume was 4 billion pieces. In the succeeding seventy years it has multiplied fifteen times, and is still growing. Our studies indicate, furthermore, that by 1985, when, the Bureau of the Census estimates, there will be 304 million persons in the United States, mail volume will be thirty-seven times greater than it was less than one hundred years before, and the postal service will handle a per capita average of 485 pieces per year.

What demands will that create? We shall look at that fantastic future later. For the present, it is enough to glance at the current problems and incredible achievements of our postal service. Running it almost requires combining the black art of gazing into a crystal ball with the mathematics of electronic calculation, for of all the major businesses in the world, the Post Office is least able to control the demands made upon it; it simply must meet them.

Furthermore, under archaic practices of financing, it must guess the public demand up to a year and a half in advance and then, without control of its rates or its payroll expenses, operate on a Congressional appropriation.

It may come as a surprise to many that all the receipts of the Post Office Department are paid directly into the Postal Fund of the Treasury of the United States and are not available for expenditure by the Department except to the extent that appropriations are made by the Congress. As a result, the Postmaster General faces serious difficulties in managing the financial problems of the Department, often finding it impossible to avoid serious interruptions in postal service when mail volume exceeds estimates on which appropriations were based.

Such a difficulty occurred in 1957 when the Appropriations

Committee of the House of Representatives, ignoring the recommendations of the Department, cut the postal appropriation so drastically as to necessitate a severe reduction of services, which proved costly to business users and to the whole economy.

The Postmaster General, under the law, is subject to criminal prosecution if he spends any money whatsoever not appropriated by the Congress. Thus, when he is denied essential funds, he is in a strait jacket insofar as any adjustment is concerned. He can only close down essential services until the funds are made available.

The U.S. Post Office has as a "customer" a country building new homes at the rate of one million a year, each requiring efficient daily postal service. Cities decentralize into suburbs, and new communities with thousands of residents mushroom where cornfields stood a decade earlier.

We are called upon to distribute periodicals counting their circulation in millions and running up to two hundred pages each, or double the circulation and triple the "normal" size prior to World War II.

In the light of modern business demands for speed in delivery of mail, overnight service in metropolitan areas must be considered normal—and a time is coming when overnight delivery between any points in the continental United States will have to be achieved.

Only service agencies that must use transportation everywhere all the time are likely to be fully aware of its ever-changing nature. The public sees the drama of new air services, but cannot realize the problems of changing patterns which saw, in 1959 alone, the withdrawal of 219 mail-carrying trains from railroad schedules.

No longer is it possible to route intercity mail through intervening cities, using the larger post offices as sorting stations for the smaller cities beyond and around them. The big cities must be bypassed lest they become choked with the traffic demands upon them.

In the effort to improve services with the personnel available, mechanization becomes as important as method. It calls for the installation of near-magic machines with electronic eyes that will sort mail at the rate of thousands of pieces an hour.

It has been a long trail indeed from our prerevolutionary days when the needs of communications were served by a weekly postrider from Boston to New York, who for seventy-five cents, collect on delivery, would carry a sealed letter sheet in his leather pouch. (Consider the value of seventy-five cents in those times—a full day's pay for non-farm workers!) Or when the picturesque riders of the Pony Express, using 75 relay ponies, delivered the mail from St. Joseph, Missouri, to Sacramento, California, for postage of seven and a half dollars per letter, compared with 1960's seven-cent airmail stamp. The fastest delivery made by the famed Pony Express —over a route now requiring only five or six hours by jet airlines—took seven days and seventeen hours, a record set in carrying President Lincoln's Inaugural Address to the Pacific Coast in 1861.

The annual cash transactions of the post offices, including the sale of stamps, money orders, postal savings, and other charges for domestic services, approximate the astounding total of 20 billion dollars a year, and total disbursements of the Post Office Department exceed 4 billion dollars a year. No automobile, steel, chain-store or other private industrial company even remotely approaches such figures.

There are 32,000 regular rural mail carriers who travel more than 1,800,000 miles a day, and over 100,000 regular city carriers. The trucks needed to handle mail total 85,000, of which the Post Office Department owns 30,000 and leases or contracts for the service of 55,000 others.

The mail handled in 1959 was divided roughly as follows: 32.5 billion first-class letters, 1.4 billion airmail letters, 7 billion magazines and newspapers, 17 billion pieces of advertising matter and circulars, and 1 billion parcels, weighing nearly 6 billion pounds.

In addition to this domestic load, the Post Office Department carries as of this writing 360 million pieces of international surface mail a year and 190 million pieces of international airmail.

Finally there is the "franked mail," sent out by the Congress and "penalty mail" sent by government agencies—formerly carried "free," but now handled on the basis of payment to the Post Office from funds appropriated for this purpose. This includes 86 million pieces originating at the Congress itself, and 1.7 billion pieces of other government mail.

So much for statistics. The figures are used only to illustrate the tremendous job of the postal service—the growing job—and to point up the demands that the Post Office has been forced to meet, greatly complicated by the fact, as I have written, that the postal establishment stood still for decades, during the very period when American business was making its greatest technological progress.

Because of unrealistic postal rates that had not kept pace with rising costs, the Post Office Department was losing money at such a pace that in 1952 alone the postal deficit—money that had to be paid from the Treasury over and above postal revenues—reached an all-time high of 720 million dollars.

Nor has the Congress faced up fully to this problem as of the very date of this writing. Consider this:

From July, 1946, the first postwar budget year, to June,

1959, the entire Federal debt increased by 15.3 billion dollars. Nearly half of this astronomical sum—6.8 billion—stemmed directly from the postal deficit accumulated during those years.

Had we not been modernizing the service since 1953, the disparity between rates and costs would have caused a deficit that by June, 1959, would have sent our total Federal debt soaring well over the $300-billion-dollar mark; and equally grave, the postal establishment would have fallen so far behind the needs of the nation's growth that the result would have been little short of chaos.

It seems proper here to summarize a few of the steps that have been taken in this seven-year period, to take a quick glance at the "current inventory" in changes:

We are now past the midpoint of our projected reforms in postal-service transportation. Highway post offices, tractor-trailers, trucks, buses, and the increased use of air transport have made it possible to meet the demands of a growing population, fill the gap left by a changing railroad service and at the same time speed mail deliveries.

Billions of letters today are being delivered from twenty-four to forty-eight hours earlier than previously was possible. Next-day delivery of letters mailed within metropolitan areas is being provided to 150 million Americans living in 90 metropolitan areas of the country.

Newly built modern post-office buildings have improved operations in 4,300 locations in the last seven years *without incurring a cent of construction costs for the taxpayer.* We are using a commercial-type lease system that actually costs the Post Office Department *less per square foot* for occupancy than the program of public works construction with appropriated Federal funds.

Three new post-office buildings *are being added every*

working day, and these are truly modern buildings—efficient and comfortable for the public and postal workers.

Behind the scenes in postal operations is the economical equipment used by businesses that must account for every penny of costs—modern conveyors, lift trucks, tying machines, label-printing machines, and many other devices new to postal operation. When vehicles are purchased, they are bought on the basis of use and need. As an instance of older practice our engineers found that one familiar type of mail truck was still being built to archaic specifications that made it six times as strong, and far more expensive, than necessary to meet any demands upon it. That is an example of inexcusably wasteful red tape.

To a degree we may say great programs have been started to improve the handling of mail at every step from the selling of a postage stamp to delivery of a letter.

When I first went into the Post Office Building in Washington after my appointment as the fifty-fourth Postmaster General and was ushered into the spacious, ornate office I have occupied since 1953, I felt as alone as a solitary boy in a drill hall; and in this lonely atmosphere, I was not long in realizing that if any Presidential directive were to be followed, I must be able to call upon men of experience with a record of leadership in the business world.

I was successful in obtaining such support and, moreover, the men who came from important positions in business and industry to join me became as sharply inspired by the United States Post Office story as did I. It is this challenging story that I want to tell you now.

3

An Epic in Pioneering

The United States Post Office system is a *federal* service for all citizens, with no interference or control to be exercized over it by any state. Three stout legs of its origin have supported this status through the years.

First, the Continental Congress established postal services for the North American Colonies by an act passed on July 26, 1775, superseding, even before the Revolution, the comparable service operated under the British Crown.

Second, the service was authorized in the Constitution, with the single sentence, "The Congress shall have power . . . to establish post-offices and post-roads."

Third, the independent nation, acting through Congress,

passed the first United States postal act in 1789, and President Washington appointed the first Federal Postmaster General, to supervise a service that then embraced about two thousand miles of post roads and seventy-five postmasters.

Behind that chronology lies a story of conflict and human interest—particularly affecting Benjamin Franklin—that is one of the great epics of pioneering. Our first postal service was unique in its freedoms and responsibilities, but like religion and politics it reflected an evolution of experiment and imagination that had stirred men's minds for centuries.

Information, communication of ideas, and the spread of "news" either by manuscript or the printed word had intrigued all but the most insular minds down through the ages.

In 1672 there already existed in England an official "Master of the Postes," who supervised a loosely knit postal organization. His office awakened to the fact that two of the cities in the American Colonies required some official method of communicating with each other, after the pattern then operating in a primitive manner in Europe. Orders were sent to Governor Loveland of the New York Colony to set up a mail service "to goe monthly" between New York and Boston.

How it worked, or whether it worked at all, is a mystery lost in time, but in 1677 the General Court of Massachusetts, acting on a petition filed by some Boston merchants, formally appointed John Hayward, identified as "the Scrivener," to accept and convey to specified addresses letters given to him. He had the start of a good business, as he set his own fees, hired his own helpers, and in fact enjoyed on a small scale a monopoly like that of the Count of Thurn and Taxis, in Germany, whose family held the German postal service as a hereditary right.

William Penn, the foresighted proprietary Governor of Pennsylvania, established a post office in Philadelphia in July,

1683, and appointed Henry Waldy as postmaster, with authority "to supply passengers with horses from Philadelphia to New Castle, or to the Falls of Delaware, and to send a weekly mail between said places, the times of departure thereof to be carefully published on the meeting-house door and in other public places."

The thrifty Quaker thus set two examples for the modern mails—use of transportation that had other means of support, and regular schedules. Soon thereafter Penn extended his colony's post service to other routes connecting Philadelphia with other towns in Pennsylvania and Maryland.

There was, however, no post linkage along the "backbone" of the Colonies, from north to south.

In 1692, the Virginia General Assembly attempted to fall into this line of postal development, appointing Thomas Neale as Postmaster General, but his service failed because of the dispersed nature of Virginia's settlements.

Each of these early postal routes was covered by riders on horseback, served by remount stations at varying intervals. The routes were for the most part Indian trails, following natural contours of rivers and shore lines; the riders' principal protection was their own training in survival, as most of the Indians and many settlers held scant respect for the sanctity of the mail. The doubtfulness of delivery supplied the principal reason for the system of payment on receipt, rather than on posting, of mail.

In 1700, the British Government authorized Colonel John Hamilton, of New Jersey, to set up a continental postal system, again on the private-contract basis, giving him a monopoly supposed to run for twenty-one years. How he fared in profits is not known, but the monopoly was canceled in 1710 when the British Parliament, during Queen Anne's reign, established the first truly national postal system and embraced the American Colonies in the pattern.

By 1711 there was weekly mail between Boston and Maine, and fortnightly mail between Boston and New York. By 1717 there was weekly mail service from New York to Williamsburg, Virginia, also serving Philadelphia en route; and in 1727 the principal pattern of the day was rounded out by inauguration of fortnightly service between Philadelphia and Annapolis, Maryland. Independent Colonial efforts to establish postal services ceased, and in the American Colonies resided a Deputy Postmaster General who reported directly to the Postmaster General in London.

The dignity of postal service, on a par with that of other important arms of government, was certified by the 1710 British statute which prescribed that the Postmaster General should be a peer of the realm, a member of the Privy Council and generally a Cabinet Minister.

So the beginnings of a postal system developed in America and so was created an office with which Benjamin Franklin, although always active in many other fields, was to be connected for almost forty years.

At thirty-one years of age, Franklin was already a busy adopted son of Philadelphia, where he had made a considerable financial success with two publications, the newspaper *Pennsylvania Gazette* and the periodical *Poor Richard's Almanac*. But he was not too busy to accept, or seek out, in 1737, the additional job as postmaster at Philadelphia, and to participate in laying the foundations of the American postal service. In addition to his local duties, he was given an assignment by the Deputy Postmaster General for the Colonies to regulate the activities of the entire Colonial postal service and to set up accounting procedures for postmasters.

In 1753 two men were appointed co-jointly as Deputy Postmaster General, Franklin and William Hunter, and Franklin kept his post until the eve of the Revolution. His record over the next twenty-five years indicates that he held a political sinecure, since he was absent so much of the time, but on the credit side he with Hunter built up the postal service to a point where it provided three times as much postal revenue for the Royal Exchequer as did Ireland with its concentrated rural population and much larger city populations.

Actually, during his term of office, Franklin was in Britain more than he was in the Colonies, on the long series of diplomatic missions that culminated during the Revolution in his Ministership to France.

With his usual foresight, however, he made sure of at least one point of postal policy: he backed with all his vigor the tradition of freedom and sanctity of the mails that was to make correspondence—even letter writing that was disloyal or treasonable in the view of the British Crown—possible in the hectic days of 1774 and 1775, when the Committees of Correspondence were transmitting to each other plans that would have brought them to the gallows if discovered.

Then, in 1774, the wrath of the crown descended on Franklin while he was in London. He was dismissed from his office as American Deputy Postmaster General through what he termed "a freak of the minister's," or spite on the part of the Postmaster General. Part of the cause lay in testimony Franklin had given during an investigation of the conduct of Governor Hutchinson of Massachusetts. Part was due, it seemed, to discovery of the strong support that the now venerable sage, scientist, and diplomat was giving to the cause of independence. A few months later Franklin sailed for home.

On July 26, 1775, only a year after his dismissal in disgrace by the British Postmaster General, Franklin was appointed Postmaster General by the Continental Congress, with virtually unlimited authority to establish an independent American postal system.

His salary was set at 1,000 dollars a year and he was authorized to hire a secretary and a comptroller at 340 dollars per year each. In only sixteen months in that office, Franklin reorganized his former royal service, and on being called to more active work in political support of the Revolution in November of 1776, he turned the office over to Richard Bache, his son-in-law, who held it throughout the Revolution and until 1782.

It was less what Franklin did in his sixteen months of Federal office than what he had done in almost forty years of Colonial service that caused him to be recorded as "Father of the United States postal service."

After the Revolution the Continental Congress passed an act combining into one law all the authorizations made before, and following the pattern of Franklin's thinking. These in effect proposed that postal revenues should be used exclusively for the improvement of service, establishment of new post offices, and the support of ships to supplement the overland transport of mail. Postriders were authorized to carry newspapers, which were then generally single sheet in size. The salaries of postmasters were not to exceed one fifth of their revenues.

However, after 1782, and almost to the time of the adoption of the Constitution in 1789, business was so stagnant and the average individual so poor that the postal service was the "poor relation" of the Government. Business never exceeded thirty-five thousand dollars a year and in 1789 amounted only to twenty-five thousand. Then the boom, and consequent development began.

It would be a dramatic story, I am sure, to be able to state here that, with the postal service happily established as one of the very foundations of the new free American society, it thereafter bloomed like a rose in the garden of freedom. The contrary, however, seems to be the case, as is apparent to anyone who has waded through the infinite details of the beginnings of our Post Office Department.

As in almost every other factor of growth in our free society there first existed, of course, the idea. But ideas are too apt to be only intangible things—confined to debates in meetings or embalmed in forgotten papers—unless energetic individuals grapple with them and wrestle them into shape.

Franklin's son-in-law, Bache, kept a minute record of the money he spent during his postmastership, but there are virtually no other records of how the postal service fared up to the time he resigned in 1782, and was succeeded by Ebenezer Hazard, who in 1775 had been Postmaster at New York. The change-over from Bache (appointed under nepotism) to Hazard meant little more than a change of name and face at the Post Office desk in Philadelphia. The Continental Congress passed a series of amendments to the older Colonial postal laws, but energy still was lacking, possibly because of denigration of the service to the status of a bureau within a department.

The postal service was simply an arm of the Treasury Department, at a time when establishment of sound money and payment of the debts incurred in the Revolution were the all-engrossing duties of the Treasury. To a Department wrestling with dollar problems counted in millions, the postal service's importance is best illustrated by the record that as late as 1789 mail was carried over routes totaling only two thousand miles, that services were available in only seventy-five post offices and that the entire operation had to be financed out of revenues of twenty-five thousand dollars. A score of contractors carried the mail over these routes—ending in the North at Wiscasset, Maine, and in the South at Savannah, Georgia.

The entire service was denounced for its inadequacy by Samuel Osgood, of Massachusetts, who was appointed Postmaster General by George Washington (the first under consti-

tutional government) in September, 1789. Although Osgood
was subordinate to the Secretary of the Treasury, Alexander
Hamilton, he evidently held the necessary authority and had
the required energy to start the postal department humming
on its way to becoming a truly national service.

In the next eight years, Osgood and his one successor under
Washington, Timothy Pickering, multiplied postal operations
six times and assisted the President and the Congress in evolving, in 1784, a completely new Federal law that has been
termed the first postal law of a permanent character.

Within the limits possible, these two Postmasters General
set up the first standards of efficiency, replaced the Colonial
patronage system with one under which postmasters were selected more on the basis of integrity and efficiency, and strove
to speed up service. In 1785, in fact, the Postmaster General
had received Congressional authority to use stagecoaches to
supplement mounted men in carrying the mail, but as long as
mail carriage was confined to unpaved roads and horse-drawn
vehicles, the pace was still that of a snail.

Nevertheless, although speed had to wait on future inven-
tions, other things of great importance right down to the present were being done by energetic men. Osgood was such a
man. In January of 1790 he wrote a report to Hamilton which
the latter sent on to the House of Representatives, and which
stands today as a classic of constructive suggestions. The report contained six blunt "observations" with a host of suggestions for correcting the errors that Osgood saw:

> First. That there may be so few letters written that, un-
> der the best regulations, it would not amount to anything
> considerably; and the dispersed manner of settling the coun-
> try may operate powerfully against the productiveness of
> the Post Office.
> Second. The franking of letters may have been extended
> too far.

Third. Ship letters (foreign mail then handled privately) may not have been properly attended to.

Fourth. The rate of postage may have been too high in some instances, and too low in others.

Fifth. Stage drivers and private postriders may have been the carriers of many letters which ought to have gone in the mail.

Sixth. The Postmasters may have consulted their own interest in preference to the public.

Here was truly a Yankee with a long nose for chicanery, smelling it out for the benefit of the public service. He had many ideas to offer.

He frankly stated that no one could control Point Number One, but implied that if the service otherwise was brought up to par, there would be plenty of business to finance development of an efficient service.

And in a year when postal revenues and costs had been less than twenty-five thousand dollars he forecast a time when the Post Office would have a revenue of five hundred thousand dollars a year, on ten million letters at an average postal return of five cents each or on half that number at ten cents each. But he added with Yankee realism that "a more energetic system" would be required to produce even a fifth of that sum.

This would mean, he said, that in servicing a three million population scattered over a "great extent of territory" many new routes would have to be established, the mail corrected of abuses through carriage by unauthorized persons and the sums due on delivery sufficiently collected. All mail was as yet C.O.D. On the last point Osgood estimated that half of the money due the Post Office was not coming in, either because letters were not accepted by addressees, or collections were being pocketed by the carriers.

He suggested several new procedures requiring legislation:

1. Revision of postal rates based on average costs per mile

—a practice later adopted but subsequently discontinued. In this case, he sought to make undercutting of prices by illegal carriers unprofitable.

2. More stringent regulation of postmasters and postriders in the matter of handling business and keeping to schedules. Many were slothful and careless, he said, and he charged also that many postriders were carrying both letters and newspapers privately, charging for these to their own profit.

3. Finally, Osgood flew in the face of "democratic" precepts of his own time by recommending that postmasters be appointed on the basis of responsibility demonstrated in their communities; that the system of letting out mail contracts to the lowest bidders resulted in the mail being handled by "poor people" who were unable to carry out their contracts.

But Osgood did not confine himself to writing reports. With the evidently enthusiastic backing of President Washington, he picked three lieutenants to work in strategic spots. First was Jonathan Burrall, his personal assistant, who was immediately sent to reform the services in the South where regularity of dispatch was unknown. Sebastian Bauman was named postmaster at New York, then the leading seaport and the relay station to New England. At home, in Philadelphia, where apart from the Federal post office, the local work load also included the transit of all north-south posts, Robert Patton was named as postmaster.

Finally, Osgood advised the assessment of a small charge for the carrying of newspapers, ranging from one to one and one-half cents each, to be paid in advance and one half of the receipts to be retained by postmasters for their trouble. This financial inducement to postmasters to collect newspaper postage in advance was great, as they were permitted to keep only one fifth of letter postage, out of which they paid their own expenses.

By this action, Osgood established the first prepaid postage, a development half a century ahead of prepaid and stamped letter mail, and set the precedent for a preferential rate for newspapers which has held to the present time. Within two years this recommendation was passed into law by the Congress.

As the result of Osgood's pioneering work and Timothy Pickering's extension of his energy and efficiency, the end of George Washington's Administration in 1795 saw the number of post offices increased in eight years from 75 to 453, the length of post routes in regular mail service increased from 2,000 to 13,207 miles, and postal income jumped from $25,000 to $160,620. Percentage-wise, that record of gain would be hard to match at any time.

The eighteenth century rounded out Post Office history with Joseph Habersham, of Georgia, acting throughout President John Adams' single term of office and increasing postal routes to 20,817 miles in 1800, the total of post offices to 903 and annual postal revenues to $280,804. Truly the postal service was on its way, with a firm foundation laid for extension and development, but needing most of all new ways to speed the mail. There still was lacking, too, a code of ethics and efficient policing to guard the sanctity of the mail.

Today when we strive to cut hours off cross-continental delivery times, it seems hard to believe how slow the mails were when horses' legs were the sole means of transportation. At the turn of the nineteenth century forty days were required to obtain an answer in Portland, Maine, to a letter addressed to Savannah, Georgia, and forty-four days must elapse for a round-trip communication between Philadelphia and Nashville, Tennessee.

The wait for better transport methods would be thirteen years, by coincidence the exact length of time that the office of Postmaster General was held by Gideon Granger, of Connecticut, appointed by Thomas Jefferson in 1801, and dismissed by James Madison in 1814 as a result of a political argument.

Granger was so efficient in handling the postal business, and building up a substantial profit on it, that Jefferson—usually a stickler for service in the public interest regardless of cost to the Treasury—seriously considered earmarking the "postal profits" as a means of paying off the national debt. What an enticing but illusory concept as we look at it today! Our President and I have, indeed, repeatedly urged the Congress to help put the service on a break-even basis.

While the business of the mail was growing in the 1790's, two historic precedents in personnel operations came into being as part of postal legislation. One was the appointment of a woman postmaster, first of a whole subsequent sisterhood, in 1792, a time when this was probably the only professional work open to a respectable woman.

The other was a vital change in the laws guarding the sanctity of the mails. Up to 1799, the single penalty in the law for "interrupting the safety of correspondence" was death. Habersham noted that the punishment was so severe that it could not be enforced; juries and courts refused to convict in the face of a penalty hung over from the crueler days of the Middle Ages.

In a report to Congress, he discussed imprisonment as an alternative, but noted that "from the number of respectable, but unfortunate debtors, with which the public gaols are crowded, imprisonment has almost ceased to be a scandal."

As an alternative he suggested, and the Congress passed as law, the substitute penalty of flogging, with capital punishment being kept as legal for second offenders.

Thus, the foundations of the postal service were laid by 1800. Henceforth its growth would be meteoric in terms of decades, as it kept in step with parallel population growth and industrial development of the United States.

U.S. MAIL

No other country on earth offered like opportunities or the challenge of distance or the demands of a free society. The United States postal service would come to a point where it excelled all others in volume and variety of public services.

But let it be clearly stated here—as will be repeatedly acknowledged—that we were not always first.

4

"She Rides Horseback
and Carries a Revolver"

It was inevitable that the question should arise and have to
be settled: Should the United States have its own means of
carrying the mails, or let common carriers do the job? There
were farsighted and inquiring minds studying the question of
government ownership of public utilities even in 1802.

It is interesting to speculate as to what might have developed had the Government built its own carrier network over
the past 150 years, but it is also idle, since the decision did not
go in that direction.

In any event, when the question arose, it led to creation of
a major precedent in American Government history, as well

as leaving to us a rare insight into the cost of travel and transportation at the time.

The question was raised by Senator James Jackson, Chairman of "the Committee of the Senate of the Post Office Establishment." Senator Jackson noted that the Government was operating its own wholly-owned line between Philadelphia and Baltimore, and asked for a report by Gideon Granger on the probable cost and problems of direct operation of other routes when the current contracts expired in 1803 and 1804.

Granger reported in meticulous detail that establishment of the public line from Philadelphia to Baltimore, a distance of 103 miles, had cost $10,567.37 for horses, carriages and harness, the horses averaging $132.40 each and the carriages an average of $376.74 each. He did not give the costs of salaries and upkeep.

The main route services then, in the winter of 1802, included nine under private contract, some designated as "double-line," or with simultaneous two-way traffic, and some "single-line." These routes totaled 1,819 miles of highways, of which 449 were double, making 2,268 operating mileage.

Granger's figures showed that to set up government-owned service of those routes would require sixty "carriages" and 515 horses, costing $90,790.12, plus wages of riders and drivers, maintenance of equipment and keep for the horses, at a time when the Government was able to contract the entire Portland, Maine-Louisville, Kentucky service for a total of $29,882 a year.

Averages from these figures show that the mails in 1802, carried only on the main post roads, thus required approximately 500 horses for less than 2,500 miles of route. The "good old days" certainly were not cheap either in the terms of present dollars or of dollars of 150 years ago which had ten times the purchasing power of today's!

In 1810, when the post routes were consolidated into a

single service under uniform private contracts, American letter postage was revised to a bracket of rates ranging from eight
to twenty-five cents each for single-sheet letters, according to
the distance carried, while newspapers distributed within the
state where they were published paid a uniform one-cent rate.

By that time the experiment by the Post Office in handling
mail in government-owned equipment had been abandoned
in the face of arguments that such "vast" government operations would entail untold patronage, perplexity and responsibility. Perhaps the fact that the Post Office cleared eleven
thousand dollars profit in three years of operating the Phila-
delphia-Baltimore route seemed to indicate too fruitful a
source of temptation for civil employees. These handled (and
under government operation would control) fortunes in relation to their salaries.

While these debates progressed, moreover, new and faster
means of transportation were coming into being.

The steam engine had been made practical, and the reliability of the first paddle-wheel steamers as common carriers was
proven on the nation's inland waterways.

When the War of 1812 began, the Post Office was probably
the largest single business operation in the United States.
Despite the upsets of the economy, the service continued to
grow, although receipts would have fallen drastically had not
all postage rates been increased temporarily by 50 per cent in
the years 1813 and 1814.

By 1815, the first year of peace, the post offices numbered
an even three thousand and revenues reached more than
$1,043,000, supporting 43,966 miles of post roads. Now the
Postmaster General was Return J. Meigs, of Ohio, and while
postmasters still worked on commission, some did so much
business that their incomes had been limited by law in 1810
to a maximum of two thousand dollars per year.

43

And important beyond all expectation was the new development of fast water carriage of the mails by steamboat.

In 1813, the Congress passed a law declaring waterways to be "post routes," and authorized the Postmaster General to use as mail carriers any packets plying them, so long as contract rates paid to steamship companies were no greater than those paid to land contractors on parallel routes. This one act hastened the carrying of mail on water routes at a speed far beyond the average pace of coaches on muddy roads or the forty miles a day traveled normally by relays of mounted riders on narrow trails.

Just when the first sealed leather pouch of mail was put aboard a high-stacked, smoke-belching, wood-burning river steamer has been lost from the records, but it was sometime in 1813 or 1814 and the steamer plied between New Orleans, Louisiana, and Natchez, Mississippi. John B. Furay, a post-office inspector, entered such a note in his diary, plus the information that the contract by the Government allowed the steamboat a rate of six cents per letter.

Very soon thereafter canal boats entered the picture. These were barges drawn by horses that plodded along the tow paths. There was one such "pioneer route" between Norfolk, Virginia, and Elizabeth City, North Carolina—possibly the first of its kind—for which there is a record covering the year starting January 1, 1816. This was experimental. It was not until 1836, in fact, that canals were declared to be "post roads."

Slow as water transport was, it was at least steady and except for extraordinary occasions it took carriage of the mail out of two hazards—mud and banditry on remote roads. Yet most of the mail would travel for almost twenty-five years more by the traditional slow-gaited methods. Railroads would not become official mail carriers, or "post roads," until a law was passed by the Congress in 1838. In 1813, we must remember, although the steam engine was proven, fast-powered rail-road and highway transport were as much a dream of the future as would be today's airmail at the time the Wright brothers made their first flights at Kitty Hawk.

The actual growth of water transport in its earliest years cannot be traced, as all postal contract payments were reported in lump sums. However, by 1843, when costs were segregated, there were 5,792 miles of water routes along the rivers, on which mail-carrying steamers were collecting almost $265,000 in contract fees.

As for costs to letter writers, the 50-per-cent increase imposed in 1813 and 1814 was repealed in 1815, but in 1816, new and heavier charges went into effect and remained unchanged for twenty-nine years. They were one-sheet letters: not over thirty miles, six cents; not over eighty miles, ten cents; not over one hundred and fifty miles, twelve and a half cents; not over four hundred miles, eighteen and three-quarter cents; greater distances, twenty-five cents.

Letters of two or more sheets paid additional postage in proportion and, if one weighed more than one ounce, the postage was quadrupled. These rates were steep, and make present prices for incomparably speedier services appear to be the world's best bargain—which, in fact, they are.

Newspapers still were carried for one cent each within a state, but paid one and one-half cents outside. Magazines and pamphlets were charged one and one-half cents within states and two and one-half beyond if prepaid, but if not prepaid the circulars rate jumped to four and six cents respectively. Communication was a luxury, indeed.

Doubtless, however, when complaints were made as to costs, the postmasters of that day could begin to reply, with honesty, "But look at the service."

In fact, the service was getting to the point where Postmaster Meigs became the first seriously to suggest cutting down of services in the "loss areas," where money collected did not pay the costs of service.

As the web of postal routes and services spread through the first thirty years of the nineteenth century, there came a realization—gradual at first but later in overwhelming measure—that this was the prime service of the Federal Government.

Primitive though the means at hand might have been, they were great for the times. In 1820 the number of post offices reached forty-five hundred. Just five years later there were one thousand more, and finally Congress did a simple yet eloquent thing in recognition of what this all meant.

In 1827, in the Administration of John Quincy Adams, while John McLean was Postmaster General, the salary of that office was set at six thousand dollars. This was the same salary paid to other Cabinet members—then including only the Secretaries of State, Treasury, and War.

The Postmaster General and the service he represented thereupon moved out of the status of a section of the Treasury Department, where the postal service formerly had been "pigeonholed," and acquired its own entity, which it since has retained.

Behind the façade of swelling statistics of route miles, offices and revenues, there also was growing up the very personal side of the postal service—its people, with their long traditions and responsibilities.

Then, as today, it was a service of "public trust" and no inconsiderable individual responsibility, because we must remember that postal service was still a "collect" service. Each individual postmaster collected the receipts on letters sent to his post-office customers; normally he paid the expenses of his own office and of local hired services on his own responsibility.

In the end he made meticulous reports, his accounts were "surveyed" by inspectors, and finally all the paper work of a day in which there were no adding machines, typewriters or other mechanical aids, wound up in Washington.

Then also, it seemed that an act of Congress was required to make the slightest change, or to correct the smallest error.

While thinking of this period, I picked up a volume of State Papers and thumbed through some of the reports to the Congress in the session of 1830. These have a strangely familiar ring. As examples:

> Illinois is petitioning for improvement of a post road at Federal expense.
>
> The States of Indiana and Illinois jointly ask for improvement of the post road running between Louisville, Kentucky, and St. Louis, Missouri.
>
> Peter Dox, the postmaster at Albany, New York, is still troubled over disallowance of $1,478.35 of his claims for expenses in the year 1815 [when his total receipts were $8,792.89] and steps are being taken to pass a "relief bill" taking this charge off his back.
>
> Fielding L. White, jailer for Madison County, Alabama, is seeking recovery of a fifty-dollar reward he paid in 1828 for the recapture of an alleged mail robber named David H. Dyer, who had been arrested and put into his custody. Although Dyer later escaped, White thought the reward was suitable and paid it, but no law authorized it. Congress did reimburse him.
>
> Josiah H. Webb in 1805 [years prior to this time] was shot and permanently disabled while carrying the mail through the Creek Nation, from Fort Stoddert to Athens, Georgia. After twenty-five years, Webb was receiving the customary pension of fifty dollars a year paid to mail carriers permanently invalided in service. Congress had held hearings on the case of the aging mail veteran and voted that his pension hereafter would be ninety-six dollars a year, or the same as that paid to enlisted soldiers disabled on duty.

It is both startling and heart-warming to realize the degree to which the service had opened careers for women by 1830.

And this in a day when as yet private and public business had few or no women clerks; when, in fact, the woman who must earn her own keep in a "respectable" manner was limited to occasional schoolteaching or more generally to menial work or the lower-paid jobs in shops.

If we search for a reason for the unique social character accorded to postal service for women, it seems to be that this service was essentially a "home service." Except for a few larger centers, the postmaster carried out his responsibility from his house or more generally the building in which he both kept store and raised his family.

Most of the early postmasters were storekeepers. Their places of business were the community centers. They knew everyone in town and the surrounding countryside. They were respected. They knew something of elementary account-keeping. Having property, they were responsible and could be bonded.

Usually every member of a postmaster's family was involved in running his postal affairs as well as his business, as there were no set hours and no days off. The mail was sorted for delivery as soon as it arrived. Mail was accepted when deposited.

In 1830, as a matter of fact, there was long and contentious debate in Congress over petitions from "blue law" advocates for Sunday closing of all post offices. In the end, the effort failed, with the compromise that post offices should close during hours of church worship, but that posts arriving on Sunday should be distributed an hour thereafter.

There was far more to running the post office of early days than the sorting of mail and collection of postage. Provision had to be made for feeding and "refreshment" of horses and drivers, and this meant kitchen work. Putting up drivers and riders overnight added innkeeping to the postal chores. This was woman's work. Hence women automatically came into

48

the postal picture almost from the dawn of the service. In the postal field, probably first of all, there came a recognition that women could be trusted with responsibilities—a revolutionary conclusion indeed in the eighteenth century.

Perhaps the pattern was set in the United States by the utter respectability of the first woman to hold such a job—a "proper Bostonian" and a sister-in-law of Benjamin Franklin. Incidentally this was also a clear-cut case of the nepotism that was to dog the American postal service for almost two hundred years until abolished in our own generation.

Benjamin Franklin, having become Postmaster General for the American Colonies, appointed his brother, John Franklin, as postmaster in Boston in 1754.

The Boston postmastership was a profitable one, but John did not live long to enjoy its patronage. He died in January of 1756. Thereupon his widow was appointed to succeed him. Mrs. John Franklin became not only the first woman postmaster in America but, according to researches reported by Carl Van Doren in his biography of Benjamin Franklin, the "first woman to hold public office in America." Evidently she did well, for no criticism of her service has been found.

Almost twenty years later, Miss Mary K. Goddard was appointed postmistress at Baltimore in 1775. Her first warrant was issued from the Continental Post Office, and she survived all the changes of the next twenty-five years.

An old ledger in the Post Office Department Library shows that an Elizabeth Creswell was postmistress at Charlestown, Maryland, in 1786.

The distinction of appointment as first woman postmaster after adoption of the Constitution—although she was outranked in seniority by these hold-overs—went to Mrs. Sarah DeCrow, whose appointment on September 27, 1792, is recorded in the current letter books of the Postmaster General. But the records neglect to name her city. The distinction was nonetheless a marked one because in 1792, with the great flurry of new patronage jobs that came with stabilized government, Mrs. DeCrow was one among the 195 postmasters in the whole United States.

Only two years later, the role of women in the postal service opened into a new field—that of cross-country courier—at a time when records indicate this to have been hazardous work.

On December 29, 1794, the sketchy old records show that papers were forwarded for execution by Mrs. Ann Blount, giving her a contract to carry the mail from Edenton to Indiantown, North Carolina, in what then was remote frontier country mainly inhabited by roving Indians and wild animals.

A description of the Post Office Department written in 1893 by Marshall Cushing recorded that there then were 6,335 postmistresses. He added the note that in a nationwide inspection of postal services these women "came grandly to the front."

And women carried the mail outdoors, too, in those latter days that still retained the aura of pioneering times. Examples from Cushing's observations:

> Mrs. Clara Carter, of West Ellsworth, Maine, drives the mail coach from that place to Ellsworth, seven miles away. A Lewiston *Journal* correspondent, who recently made the trip with her, saw her deliver twelve packages and as many letters, besides several papers, along the route, attend to errands and look after two passengers, all in one hour and twenty minutes.
>
> This energetic woman rises early in the morning, does the cooking for five in the family, starts at seven for the city with the mail and numerous errands that are given to her without memoranda. She returns at noon, gets dinner, goes to the blueberry fields and picks ten quarts of berries or more in the afternoon, and in the cool of evening does the family washing and ironing and other household tasks. This amount of work she performs six days in the week, varying

the routine in the afternoon, out of berry season, by sewing for the family. She finds time, too, to play on the parlor organ an hour or more in the evening, or to entertain visitors.

One wonders, where was Mr. Carter?

Jumping across the country in his description of women carriers, Cushing noted:

> There is a brave little woman mail carrier in Oregon. She travels from the head of navigation on Siuslaw's River over the Coast Range Mountains, and then follows the river through Hale's post office within fifteen miles of Eugene City. Her route is twenty miles long, and right in the heart of the mountains. She carries a revolver. Miss Westman is a plump brunette, twenty-two years old. Her father and uncle operate a stage line. At Hale's station the young woman meets her father and takes the mail to Eugene City.
>
> Miss Westman has never met with a mishap. On one of her trips last year she found three good-sized bears in the road, right in front of her. The horse became frightened, threw his rider and ran back. Miss Westman started after the runaway, remounted, and rode right through the savage line, and, strange to say, she was not attacked. Some friends later went to the place and killed the bears.

However much sentiment for the postal service was being nurtured in the early nineteenth century, the organization faced mounting criticism that even in the days of slow communication was rasping on Washington's official ears.

The service was unbelievably slow for the expanding economy of the country. Rates were burdensomely high. The red tape involved in having every postmaster be in effect a private monopoly was cumbersome. And despite continuing improvements in service, the mails were uncertain.

Americans acquainted with Europe—and a surprising number were cosmopolite in their outlook—made invidious comparisons. They overlooked the fact that all national postal services in Europe were confined to relatively small areas, but their complaints registered with effect. And to top it all, there were suspicions that the American postal service was not only inefficient but wasteful.

The smell of reform was in the air, and changes came quickly; not always permanent, but changes that radically transformed the postal service through the years between 1836 and 1846.

It all began with the discovery in 1835, during President Andrew Jackson's administration, that under Postmaster General William T. Barry the financial affairs of the postal service had come undone at the seams. There was no allegation of crookedness, but suddenly the formerly profitable postal service was in arrears to the Treasury for large sums of money, contractors were not receiving their pay, and the Post Office Department dipped so low financially that it sought loans from commercial banks to pay its debts.

With a fine gesture of courtliness, President Jackson, under political pressure from the newspapers and the Congress, gently "kicked upstairs" the amiable Mr. Barry with an appointment as Minister to Spain. The President named Amos Kendall, then the Fourth Auditor of the Treasury Department (and watchdog over Post Office finances) as Postmaster General. Kendall, between May of 1835 and October of 1837, paid off all the Post Office debts, improved the service and created a surplus of $780,000 in the Post Office account with the Treasury.

In the meantime, other far-reaching changes were made at Kendall's suggestion, of which a few in the legal structure continue to the present time.

One big new law was passed in 1836. Its principal effect was to take away almost dictatorial powers enjoyed by the Postmaster General and to spread out the responsibilities of his office. This was the last great major decentralization of operations prior to sweeping reforms made in the present administration to decentralize further the details handled by Washington. To the credit of the service, let it be noted here that it was Postmaster General Kendall who wrote the law embodying those early reforms, thus making him one of the great American administrators who saw the weakness inherent in his own personal power.

At the time of Kendall's induction into office, the Postmaster General alone held responsibility for letting all mail contracts. He appointed all postmasters, and adjusted and paid all accounts. Thus, in effect, the Postmaster General set up his own patronage group, was the sole judge of the type and manner of their compensation, and he could decide individually who should receive outside contracts and what the compensation should be.

The new law clipped these powers. While it left the Postmaster General full freedom of action in handling the mails, there were these significant changes:

Appointment of postmaster at offices where commissions exceeded one thousand dollars per year was placed in the hands of the President, subject to confirmation by the Senate.

All postal revenues coming to the Department at Washington were paid directly into the Treasury.

The Post Office henceforth was required to submit an annual budget anticipating expenses, which then was appropriated by the Congress.

Local postmasters were given direct responsibility for paying contractors in their areas, subject to audit by the Treasury as well as the Postal Inspection Service.

New legislation authorized "express mails," consisting of mounted men carrying pouches of letters paid for at triple rates. This service (not to be confused with the later "Pony Express" of the West) was tried on the turnpikes of the South and West, but soon was abandoned because of its cost in relationship to revenues. In any event it was outdated almost before it was established, by the new and rapid development of railroads, which in 1838 were formally designated as "post roads," and were therefore eligible to carry mail anywhere they operated.

In this period, it seems in retrospect, the Post Office Department was passing through a growing-up stage without realizing the great opportunities and responsibilities piling up for the near future with the development of the "machine age." In the evolution of all of our governmental activities, the United States was growing out of the suit of clothes tailored for a pastoral society. Fortunately, here, as in so many other cases, our Government was again proving, specifically in the case of the postal service, that the Constitution on which the structure had been built was sufficiently elastic to provide for change, while strong enough to endure as the foundation for a growing economy.

While apparently run with honesty and relative efficiency, the postal service was again in trouble in 1845. The service improvements inaugurated in 1837 had resulted in deficits to the Government, and yet rates were so high that "bootleg mail" was draining off the very revenue that the Post Office needed so badly.

Almost every passenger train operating on the now-expanding railroads carried some bags of official mail. Likewise, stagecoaches that lumbered over the networks of improved highways beyond the rail heads, and steamers and canal boats.

Nevertheless, it seemed probable that even more mail was riding illegally on each type of conveyance, either in the baggage of individuals who made a business of carrying letters at rates lower than the official postage or as "express packages" consigned to railways. Remember that it still cost from six to twenty-five cents to post a letter consisting of a single sheet of paper. Each additional sheet was charged identical additional rates; the situation was so absurd that a contemporary writer noted that the posting of a letter containing three bank notes cost the recipient (for mail still traveled C.O.D.) the price of four letters.

Adding justifiable fuel to the controversy over rates, and to the "bootlegging" practices that could not possibly be checked, was the "penny post" that had been operating in Great Britain since 1839.

Across the Atlantic Ocean, in a country whose distances did not compare with those in the United States, but where nevertheless letters might travel for six or seven hundred miles by the same types of conveyances, Rowland Hill, the British Postmaster General, had made two revolutionary changes. He had eliminated the zone method of charging for first-class mail and simultaneously reduced the rate. For the equivalent of two American cents (one English penny), an Englishman could send a letter anywhere in the country.

One easily imagines how galling this was to Americans who in 1845 paid a minimum of six cents letter postage, and with that rate good only for the first thirty miles—what is today considered as "local mail."

The new chapter of postal history, involving these and other major "reforms," became law on March 3, 1845, on the last day of President Tyler's single and otherwise undistinguished term of office, at the insistence of Postmaster General Charles A. Wickliffe, who simultaneously went out of office with the change of administration.

The omnibus postal legislation made these drastic changes:

> Reduced postage rates.
> Reformed the methods of letting mail contracts.
> Prohibited and severely penalized "bootlegging" of mail.
> Restricted the franking privilege.
> Provided machinery for regularizing and lowering the cost of foreign mail.

U.S. MAIL

Here is what each change did for, or meant to, the "new" postal concept:

Reduced postage rates: The new rates for letters applied to two categories: five cents for all letters traveling three hundred miles or less and ten cents for letters going farther. The rates covered all mail weighing not more than half an ounce, so that a letter might consist of several tissue-thin sheets and go at the standard rate for a single letter. (The present envelope with a letter enclosure had not yet come into use. Letters then, like "air letters" today, consisted of sheets of paper containing a written message on one side, and then folded and sealed with wax as glue, and addressed on the outer side.)

Reformed mail contracts: The huge losses of revenue to mail "bootleggers" were found to be due to cumbersome regulations of the Post Office Department itself, credited partly to overzealous care for security and partly to lobbying on the part of operators of stagecoaches and other passenger-carrying vehicles. The new laws brought back the man on horseback where routes were through thinly settled areas and mail volume was accordingly sparse.

The new law required the Postmaster General to grant contracts in all cases to the lowest bidders consistent with "celerity, certainty, and security," without reference to the mode of conveyance. This action hit the stage operators a hard blow, but gave the mail users and taxpayers immediate large returns.

Penalized "bootleg" mail: Ever since early Colonial days, there had been laws of one sort or another prohibiting competition of private parties with the Government in mail delivery. But the penalties were so light that enforcement had become a farce. The new law had teeth that were effective for its time: a fine of $150 for establishing private expresses on a post route for conveying any mailable matter except newspapers, pamphlets, magazines or periodicals, and a fine of $100 for private transport of such mail, to be assessed against the owners of stagecoaches, privately owned railroad cars, steamboats, packet boats or any other kind of vehicle.

As an interim note in describing these reforms, the records show immediate profit to the Government and improved mail service, plus the introduction into Post Office terminology of a new term—"Star Routes."

The improvements are matters of fascinating record considering the time when dollars were worth perhaps ten times their mid-twentieth-century purchasing power. In the first four years after enactment of these reforms, mail service was expanded by an additional 23,763 miles of routes, while the expense of carrying the mail declined by $328,000. This was quite a handsome bonus contributed by Charles Wickliffe to the Post Office and to his country in return for four years' employment at $6,000 per year.

As for the term "Star Route," the later formal name came from a punctuation mark—the use of an asterisk to indicate short-contract route names in the files.

The new laws governing letting of contracts applied only to the road carriers—stages, carriages, sulkies, and men on horseback. Rail and water routes were contracted at fixed rates established under separate laws. All other contracts were starred.

W. L. Nicholson, in 1879 the Topographer of the Post Office Department, reported that the use of the asterisks to mark bids on the services affected by the law already had become familiarly known as "star bids." And the services based on "star bids" accordingly became known as "star routes."

Restricted franking privileges: Franking of mail, or the right to send it free of postage, always has been a prerogative of the President, Cabinet members, various department officials and postmasters. The idea is to avoid all the waste involved in stamping mail that in the end would be carried free as part of governmental business.

The law of 1845 on this subject, however, was similar to more recent laws governing corporate expense accounts to the extent that it represented the first attempt to regularize such usage by requiring an accounting of the franked mail.

Still remembering that in 1845 mail was sent C.O.D., government officials generally had the right to accept communications sent to them without paying postage due. But this law required that records be kept of the amounts of postage "franked" and that the Departments and Bureaus should issue warrants "reimbursing" the Post Office for the sums involved.

The older records show that, by the mere act of requiring from officials an accounting of their use of the franking privilege, the amount of free mail was reduced materially.

However, as no rules stand still for very long—particularly in a day when political influence is potent in every governmental act—the Congress in 1847 revoked the 1845 law and, in its stead, agreed to appropriate five hundred thousand dollars a year to the Post Office Department for handling of franked mail in lieu of the accounting procedures.

It is a matter of interesting comment that although the accounting requirement was once repealed, substantially the same rules were again put into effect during the incumbency of the author of this book.

Foreign Mail: This action consisted only of authorizing the Postmaster General to make general arrangements with European continental countries for reciprocal handling of the mails; there already existed a working arrangement with Great Britain and with the Free Port of Bremen, in Germany.

Over the years there has evolved a massive series of agreements whereby any American knows that today he can post a letter to an individual in any one of some hundred countries with reasonable certainty of its being promptly delivered.

The interesting fact behind this 1845 law, however, is the observation that—in a country dedicated to the practice of making no foreign "engagements"—the Post Office was, for purely practical reasons, selected to break the ice.

Few persons realize that the oldest treaties arranging for intercourse between our own and foreign governments are the ones made soon thereafter regarding handling of the mails.

For that matter, apropos of the great attention given in recent years to the Treasury's Secret Service and to the Federal Bureau of Investigation in the Department of Justice, apparently not one American in a thousand knows that the Inspection Service of the Post Office represents a public security organization that is nearing the two-and-one-half-century mark of unbroken and unpublicized operations.

5

Security and Service

Suddenly the postal service realized that indefinite extension of routes and the search for faster transportation were not in themselves sufficient to meet public demands. Men were moving and ideas were developing. Communications, therefore, achieved an importance out of all proportion even to the record growth of population and settled areas of the United States.

As yet, in the year 1847, the postal service remained principally an extension of the ideas of the eighteenth century—basically a luxury service for carrying private letters and the conveying of newspapers and other periodicals, seldom more than a single sheet in size.

A great step had to be taken over the chasm between a

carrier organization and services suited to a "modern" society. There was insistent demand for more refinements in the existing services and for tailor-made creation of new ones.

The postal service of 1847 was traversing highways and trails throughout the entire region that has since become that part of the continental United States east of the Rocky Mountains, as far as Texas. Also, in that year California first began to receive mail service by sea around Cape Horn, and on to the Oregon Territory.

There was by that time a topographer in the Post Office Department who outlined the routes, a large staff that designated the means, and a ponderous machinery for accounting and directing this ever-growing service.

Nonetheless, the whole machinery was creaking, largely because of two factors: (1) This was still a collect service, which made all postmasters liable for collecting the revenue at each letter's destination in nickels and dimes, and (2) nothing had been done to meet the demands for special types of communications.

On July 1, 1847, the first major change in *service* as opposed to operations came into being. It emerged with the passage of a law authorizing the sale of gummed *postage stamps* to be used for prepayment of letters. Credit cannot be taken by the United States for this development. It was copied from a British practice already eight years old. But it was to change the entire character and efficiency of the sprawling system that already covered the broadest area in the world, since no other continent-wide country had any postal service worth mentioning.

It would be dramatic to report that on a certain date the mails were modernized with the issuance of stamps, but this was not the case. In fact, the first ones issued probably caused an added note of confusion to the service, even while setting an essential precedent.

Those first stamps were remarkably like the ones in use today in size, shape and engraving. The five-cent stamp (for letters traveling three hundred miles or less) was light brown in color, with a portrait of Benjamin Franklin engraved from a drawing by James B. Longacre. The ten-cent stamp, printed in black, bore a likeness of George Washington engraved from Gilbert Stuart's most famous portrait of him.

No one *had* to use the stamps when they were issued. They were a "convenience" for postmasters, many of whom already were using various types of locally printed "stamps" known as "Postmasters' provisionals."

There never had been any clear legislation or rules governing the collection of postage on letters, comparable to payment of postage on printed matter where discounts were offered as an inducement for prepayment.

The great bulk of the first-class mail still was sent collect on delivery. To the average letter writer, for whom written correspondence was then a novel experience, the collect service seemed to give assurance. Pay in advance and how could you be certain of delivery?

Yet recipients of letters did not have to accept delivery or pay postage; hence there were heavy losses by the postal service on mail transported at high contract rates but refused at the destination.

On the other hand, many letter writers—particularly businesses—desired to prepay their mail in order to relieve the addressee of the cost. This placed a special burden on local postmasters, both in marking the prepaid mail and in accounting for these receipts separately from the C.O.D. charges.

Each prepaid letter had to be marked as such by hand, with the name of the post office where it had been mailed and a notation as to the amount of postage paid by the sender. This became an intolerable burden in the larger centers, so postmasters had for some years resorted to the "provisionals," which actually were affixed to prepaid letters much as the later stamps would be.

The issuance of Federal stamps immediately eliminated the need for the "provisionals," and cut out a whole set of book-keeping operations in the local offices, as well as assuring the Federal Government of more accurate collections. The stamps issued to local postmasters were simply charged to their accounts. Payment for the stamps had only to match the value of the deliveries, so everything came out even.

In 1855 prepayment of postage was made compulsory, and henceforth the greatest headache of the service was eliminated.

Quite unforeseen was the fact that the development of the postage stamp would lay a foundation for one of the greatest modern hobbies—stamp collection. This has become so popular and so complex that it now constitutes a whole segment of Post Office Department business, and is treated here in a chapter of its own.

Despite the growing problems of postal costs to the Government, there was developing the feeling that American democracy must be served through the most economical means of dissemination of the printed word.

Newspapers were reporting news more completely. The horizons of Americans were spreading rapidly beyond their towns or counties, but even within these narrower limits news began to take on more and more meaning.

And in this field, it is notable that precedents were set by an otherwise undistinguished President who, we may assume, did a historic thing for the purpose of winning the political support of the press, which constituted his strongest opposition. The political attempt—if such it was—failed, but the precedent grew into permanent practice.

Millard Fillmore became President in July of 1850 upon the

death of President Taylor. He named Nathan K. Hall of New York, his law partner and a member of the House of Representatives, as Postmaster General. Hall's principal concern soon came to be the mounting protests against the relatively high costs of transporting printed matter through the mail—the single-sheet newspapers that still were charged from one to three and one-half cents postage.

In 1851, Hall ordered these rates cut in half if publishers prepaid the postage, and so established a precedent new in the world's postal history. It was ordered also that newspapers should be distributed free within the counties where they were published.

This single action probably accounted more than anything else for development of the county weekly, which soon became as thoroughly established a part of the American heritage as the community churches and "fresh water" colleges that marched westward in the great continental development.

As a Postmaster General in the mid-twentieth century, I may be pardoned for observing that the precedent set by Hall has remained to plague his successors. Today, when a single copy of a publication often weighs as much as the entire weekly edition of a newspaper of a century ago, the Post Office Department is faced with the fact that the average piece of second-class mail pays roughly a fifth of the cost of delivering it.

We have yet to find the proper balance between "public interest" in low rates accorded to the printed word and the postal losses involved in handling it, which inevitably must be paid by taxpayers faced with postal deficits.

This problem, I would point out, has not kept us from constant effort to improve the service for second-, third- and fourth-class mails. Many such improvements have been made in recent years—speeding delivery, simplifying regulations and procedures, and broadening the services available.

Still a third precedent of historic importance came in 1851 with a ruling that permitted the acceptance of bound books in the mail.

Prior to 1851 there had been no prejudice against the distribution of books. They simply had been too heavy for handling in the more restricted spaces afforded by highway transport. It was impossible to ask horseback riders to carry any number of these in their saddlebags.

Now, however, there had developed the means of mass handling of mail along the routes served by railroads and steamers. It was only natural that these facilities should be opened to the cultural forces represented by book publishing.

So it all started. And today the normal book selling for five dollars can be mailed anywhere in the United States usually for twelve cents in postage—the cost of sending a book which with its wrapper weighs up to two pounds.

A few years ago, in Washington, D.C., Mrs. Evalyn Walsh McLean died, and left as part of her great estate a diamond that was one of the legends of the world. Known as the "Hope Diamond," this enormous glittering bauble had been in her possession for many years. It was the center of innumerable stories, the most widespread of which was that it had brought ill fortune to each of its owners. In the case of the McLeans, the legend had grown with the tragic death in an automobile accident of a child of the family years before. But Mrs. McLean kept and wore the stone, as a pendant, until the day of her death at an advanced age.

Her estate sold it to a diamond merchant for a price reportedly more than a million dollars.

The postal service was brought into the Hope Diamond legend when its purchaser, Harry Winston, contributed the fabulous gem to the Smithsonian Institution and described in an interview how he had managed its delivery. He had simply sent it by registered mail from New York to Washington, and he added that it was normal for priceless jewels to be handled in that manner by dealers and brokers in Europe and America.

It suddenly became known, therefore, that no means of transportation is considered safer than registered mail—a fact already accepted by millions of persons consigning small articles, contracts or priceless papers every day in the year.

To the Post Office Department, the dealer's story was an interesting but not surprising bit of information. The postal service had seen many extremely valuable items transported by registered mail, including, in fact, 15 billion dollars in gold!

A fabulous chapter in the history of the registered-mail service was written when the Government decided before World War II to transfer more than 15 billion dollars' worth of gold bullion from New York and Philadelphia to the famed vaults at Fort Knox, Kentucky. The entire movement was placed under the general supervision and custody of postal inspectors.

That remarkable operation required 552 special trains, each carrying 28 million dollars of bullion. It was the world's greatest long-distance transfer of gold and was accomplished without incident. Similar shipments were made between San Francisco and Denver.

Actually, the system of registry is one of the Post Office's oldest of special "customer services," having come into operation almost immediately after prepayment of postage was made obligatory.

The registry of mail was the brain child of Postmaster General James Campbell, who served under President Franklin Pierce from 1853 through the Presidential term that ended in 1857. In 1855, Campbell suggested that Congress authorize a special system for the handling of letters containing valuable papers or small articles—specifically a means to fix responsibility for the handling at every point of change up to delivery. Registry did not originally involve insurance or reimbursement; it was simply a means for assuring maximum care.

The principal features of the plan, although elaborated and refined subsequently, remain to this day, and have been extended to cover the countries with which the United States has postal conventions.

The term "registered letter" means just what it says. When it is mailed, a receipt is given to the sender by the dispatching post office, which files a duplicate of it. When the letter reaches the addressee, a receipt for its delivery is filed with the post office of destination. The office from which it was sent is promptly notified, and the record of its safe transmission thus is made complete.

While registry marked a colorful milestone in postal services, a development in 1858 illustrated the way in which the service in general had come to be regarded virtually as sacred by the American public. In that year the first residential postal boxes were erected in major cities for the deposit of ordinary mail. To us in this day, such a development seems routine; the mailbox is as common as lights on the city streets.

Nevertheless, it is, when you stop to think of it, a remarkable demonstration of respect for an institution and of mutual trust between people.

There are, and always have been, severe penalties for robbing the mails, but no amount of penalties can ever give the assurance of security represented by the mailbox, unattended and unwatched, to which we habitually consign both our intimate messages and unregistered papers of great value, guarded only by the glue on an envelope and the symbolism of the stamp affixed to it.

6

The Pony Express

"Wanted—young skinny, wiry fellows not over 18. Must be expert riders, willing to risk death daily. Orphans preferred. Wages $25 a week. . . ."

So read a notice circulated in San Francisco in 1860. The famous transportation firm of Russell, Majors & Waddell was looking for men—or rather boys—to ride mustangs in relays on a nineteen-hundred-mile course over the most rugged and most perilous sections of the North American continent. They were preparing to start mail service via the Pony Express.

Their advertisement or other inducements obviously succeeded, for on April 3 of that year, two teenage boys leaned low over their saddle pommels, dug their heels into the flanks of their mustangs, and started from opposite terminals on the new mail run from St. Joseph, Missouri, to Sacramento, California.

What followed, over a period of eighteen months, wrote one of the glamorous pages in the history not only of the Postal Service, but of the United States.

This was the Pony Express, short lived and little more than a detail in the long history of postal development, but a stimulant to imagination that has left a deep and inspiring mark in the annals of American adventure.

The Pony Express came about because of the surging, impatient opening of America's great West. The postal service followed the covered wagons with means of communications that maintained the pioneers' contacts with the folks back home. Had this service been lacking, it is fair to assume that the development of the West would have been delayed for many years.

While some service went by ship the long way around Cape Horn, convoys of covered wagons were by 1850 carrying letters, newspapers and shipments of money to the new state of California via the Southwestern territories of New Mexico and Utah.

The convoy schedules were uncertain and they usually required at least eight weeks to make the trip. Specially trained postal inspectors guarded them, but the trips were nevertheless hazardous as the plains Indians grew more resentful of the encroachment by the white man.

Then came the bombshell that caused California to explode overnight into a great center of American life and wealth— the accidental discovery of gold at Sutter's Mill. The gold bonanza brought cascades of people, banks and businesses pouring into the West—and with them, an overwhelming demand for rapid communications with the East, a demand that could not tolerate the slow convoys and could not wait

69

for railroad construction or the extension of the telegraph. Fortunes literally depended on quick communications.

By 1860 the Post Office Department was under heavy pressure to act immediately, at any cost, to set up communications service that placed all emphasis on speed. A contractor with the ingenuity, capital, and courage to develop such a service and take the risk of operating it must be found at once.

Then it was that William H. Russell, a stagecoach operator, got together with Senator William Gwin of California in Washington and worked out the startling idea of the Pony Express. Russell gave his word to the Senator that the job would be done and went back to his partners at Leavenworth, Kansas, to get it under way.

If his partners were less than enthusiastic, it is nevertheless to their credit that the promise was carried out. Russell's only mistake was in figuring costs, because he and his partners eventually sustained a loss that was very large for that day. But in laying the groundwork for and operating the Pony Express, their record was superb.

They quickly established 190 relay stations over the nineteen-hundred-mile route. The ten miles between stations represented about the maximum that a hardy pony could be ridden at top speed without either a long rest or risk of destruction. To man these stations, Russell hired four hundred tough keepers and assistants, most of whom faced perilous existence in the wild Indian country, and several of whom paid with their lives for their jobs.

But the most important factor was the individual mail carrier, who had to be able to outrun Indian ambushers while carrying the mails through the wilderness, often through blinding snows or howling storms, in extreme heat or cold. The riders could not be big and brawny men whose weight would tire their mounts; the important weight was in the mail pouch bouncing from the saddle.

Thus the recruitment of eighty "skinny young fellows" whose weight was specified not to exceed 125 pounds—much like the jockeys who ride the race horses of today.

These young men were the almost-wild and quickly maturing products of the Western plains—many over the specified age of eighteen, but all fired with youthful lust for adventure, challenge and, not the least, spending money.

Since the speed of the run was critically dependent on the lightness of the load, the standard Western saddle was too heavy, and a modified *vaquero* which weighed but a third of the Western type was regularly used.

For a time much of the weight saved in saddlery was lost in defense hardware. The boyish pony riders bristled with revolvers, bowie knives, and at least one rifle—more armament than was usually found on armed stagecoach messengers. In time, however, the riders "thinned down" to a single pistol under orders to defend themselves by resorting to speed rather than staying to fight. The advice appears to have been sound—only one Pony Express rider was lost.

In the spring of 1860 a youngster by the name of William F. Cody was hired for a forty-five mile run. He was fifteen years old, the youngest pony rider to carry the mail. The next year he was making the run between Red Buttes and Three Crossings on the Sweetwater, a distance of 116 miles. Swooping into Three Crossings on one trip, he found that his relief rider had been killed the night before. No other rider was available, so young Cody swung the leather mail *catinas* from his spent pony to an already saddled fresh horse and rode on. Altogether, before his round trip ride was over, he had ridden 384 miles without any real period of rest!

This sturdy lad in later life was to become the world-famous "Buffalo Bill," replete in his golden years with broad-brimmed hat, flowing white hair, and goatee, and lavish accoutrement in which he appeared in his own show on tour.

Another young rider, "Pony Bob" Haslem found a string of relay stations burned and their keepers massacred by Indians, and rode a circuitous route of 380 miles to deliver safely his saddlebags of mail.

The speed of the new service was fantastic for its time. The first trip westward from St. Joseph to Sacramento was made in nine days and twenty-three hours and the reverse initial trip took eleven days and twelve hours. As the riders grew more expert and the trails more familiar, the average time for the trip dropped to eight days in summer and ten in winter.

President Lincoln's Inaugural Speech was sped westward in the record time of seven days and eleven hours, and this record was substantially matched later with news of the firing on Fort Sumter and the declaration of war in 1861.

Altogether, the Pony Express carried 30,000 pieces of mail over a total riding distance of some 650,000 miles.

At the start of the service the rate was five dollars per half ounce, but gradually the rate was reduced to one dollar per half ounce. The saddlebags largely contained letters written on onionskin paper and condensed versions of Eastern newspapers for Western readers. Also, the larger Eastern newspapers maintained correspondents at St. Joseph to collect the news arriving by Pony Express and write from it the stories to be sent eastward by rail or telegraph.

The end of the fabulous Pony Express, in fact, came when these same great facilities finally and inevitably were thrust across the Western wilderness to the coast. The last Pony Express run in October, 1861—just eighteen months after its beginning—brought forth nostalgic emotions from many who had been close to its excitement, heroism, and dedicated sense of service. In the Sacramento *Bee*, this emotion overflowed into an editorial, which read in part:

FAREWELL, PONY: . . . Farewell and forever, thou staunch, wilderness-overcoming, swift-footed messenger. . . . Thou wert the pioneer of the continent in the rapid transmission of intelligence between its peoples, and have dragged in your train the lightning itself, which, in good time, will be followed by steam communication by rail. Rest upon your honors; be satisfied with them, your destiny has been fulfilled—a new and higher power has superseded you. . . . This is no disgrace, for flesh and blood cannot always war against the elements. Rest, then, in peace; for thou hast run thy race, thou hast followed thy course, thou hast done the work that wast given thee to do.

The Pony Express passed into legend, and the roaring railroad trains and humming telegraph wires took over its task. But the Pony Express will always hold a warm place in hearts of Americans. It remains a chapter in postal history of which the postal service will always be proud.

7

In Civil War——a Revolution

In the summer of 1863, while a million men in blue and gray were fighting the still inconclusive battles of the War Between the States, a few hundred men started pioneering a service that has grown into one of the large nonmilitary "armies" in the world. These are the postmen, whose gray uniforms identify them as an essential part of the life of all American cities. Their *esprit de corps* is legendary.

Establishment of free city delivery service was one of four major actions by the Post Office Department from 1862 to 1864 that each in its way laid new foundations for today's postal service. Together they supply dramatic footnotes to a story of development that even war could not impede.

In all the biographies of Abraham Lincoln it is difficult to find mention of the contribution made by his administration to the postal service; this work was overshadowed by the stark realities of America's most tragic conflict. But the postal service benefited greatly from Lincoln's supreme capacity to delegate responsibility to his aides, once a line of action had been approved.

Montgomery Blair, a Maryland political leader, was his Postmaster General. His name has been perpetuated through "Blair House," the mansion he purchased across Pennsylvania Avenue from the White House and which in recent years has been the Government's "host house" for distinguished guests, ranging from kings and presidents to Nikita Khrushchev.

Neither Lincoln nor Blair invented or innovated great actions in the Post Office, but the latter in particular displayed a talent for responding to great ideas and developments of the time, just as today's postal-service directors constantly adapt electronics and jet-flight developments to the country's number one service enterprise.

In addition to instituting free carrier service in cities, the Civil War period saw other major developments, including: inauguration of "railroad post offices," introduction of postal money orders, and the first international postal conference.

On July 1, 1863, a few hundred postal carriers, not yet wearing uniforms, but with letter pouches slung from their shoulders, set out to revolutionize city delivery of mail in the forty-nine larger cities of the Union. They were the forerunners of a force who in time would number more than one hundred thousand letter carriers.

The "free" delivery of mail was not new, and here again it may be noted that free deliveries already had been established in some of the larger European cities. There was a great difference, however, between such deliveries in highly concentrated and congested European cities, and in the sprawling towns that made up America's cities, where distances were measured in miles rather than in rods.

In the United States there had been various types of delivery services since 1794, when a law authorized local postmasters to institute such service according to the conveniences of their areas. But the service had been expensive; in effect, it had been similar to later "special delivery" mail.

This older law authorized the hiring of mail delivery men on a fee basis—two cents for each letter delivered. In 1836, the special paid service was enlarged to include house delivery of newspapers at one cent each, and the collection of letters to be posted for a fee of two cents each.

These were luxury services, and the postal service in the 1860's no longer could be considered a luxury. In fact, Blair concluded after studying the European delivery systems, that enlargement of free services to "customers" by post offices virtually created automatic new usage that offset the cost.

While Blair was reaching these high-level conclusions, Joseph William Briggs spent many hours considering the same problem from his vantage point as a window delivery clerk in the post office at Cleveland, Ohio. He finally set down in writing a plan for the free delivery and collection of mail and took it up with the postmaster, who encouraged him to work on it.

To prove his contention and to practice details, Briggs created a route for himself and thereby became the first self-appointed modern mailman.

The Cleveland plan so impressed Blair that he appointed Briggs special agent for the installation of city free delivery service throughout the country—a job that occupied Briggs for six years and proved that in the postal service, at least, a "prophet" can receive honor in his own country and service. In 1868, Briggs also designed the first uniform worn by carriers. He died in 1872 in Cleveland, where a plaque in the post office testifies to his contributions.

From its inception free city carrier service was keyed to public demand for and support of the mail service, as shown by local postal business. It was a sort of inducement bonus, as local post offices were authorized to employ carriers only if their revenues were sufficient to support such free service. The first carriers were paid not more than eight hundred dollars a year to start—with salary increases permitted to a maximum of one thousand dollars, or approximately one fifth present pay-scale maximum in dollars.

At the end of the first year of carrier operation, 65 cities provided such service, employing a total of 685 carriers. Down through the years the service has continued (with modern improvements) so that, as recently as June 30, 1959, there were 149,000 carriers working out of 5,528 city delivery offices. The basic salary cost of the service in fiscal 1959 was $725,000,000.

While railroads were yet very primitive by modern standards, the needs of the postal service brought about a new system that—save for changes in vehicles themselves—was substantially perfected almost a century ago.

This innovation of "post offices on wheels" consisted of special mail cars that insofar as possible were complete sorting stations in themselves, as each such car is today on every long-haul mail train. Since 1941 there have been on many highways similar stations in the form of great mail trucks.

From the time that "fast" mail service via trains came into being in 1838, the postal service had been confronted with ever-increasing demands for a speed-up in handling and delivery comparable with the increased speed of transit.

Commercial mail in particular needed ever faster service. Yet when Blair became Postmaster General, there had been little or no change in handling railroad mail, which generally was carried in the same manner as on river steamers and stagecoaches.

Mail consigned from one large center to another included not only that for the principal destination but for all the satellite communities around the "railhead." As a rule, tons of mail destined for a whole county would be dumped on the platform at its county seat, and then re-sorted both for local delivery and for despatch to surrounding communities. Thus train mail that even then moved from New York to Philadelphia in four hours probably would not be delivered for some considerable time after its arrival.

On each mail train rode a "route agent," but he had time only to put off bundles at their destinations, receive others for forwarding, and keep his record of bags.

There were complaints about the service and, naturally, a great revival of "bootleg" mail service by messengers who privately carried letters requiring fast delivery.

In 1862, Blair instituted a trial "railroad post office" between Washington and New York, manning it with clerks borrowed from the larger post offices. Insofar as possible they sorted the mail according to local community destination or by area, leaving to the receiving offices only the task of sorting of their own local mail.

The experiment proved so efficient, as well as paying its own costs, that despite the pressures of war, Congress authorized the inauguration of the "railroad post office" on August 24, 1864.

There is a footnote of irony to this in the fact that the speed of air travel has reached the point today where plans to try such a system with airmail had to be abandoned because of the brief time required for trips between air terminals.

And there is further irony in the lamentable fact that declining railway service has forced more and more the abandonment of the railroad post office.

The postal money order was a "war baby" that came into being on November 1, 1864, almost too late to serve its primary purpose, but survived to become a widely used means of sending small sums of money through the mail with guaranteed safety.

Oddly enough there is no indication of a need or demand for such a service in America prior to the Civil War. Then the military services and the post office were confronted suddenly with the demand by the Army for a safe means whereby soldiers could send money home to their families.

The system of registered letters could not cope with the task involved, principally the paper work, and the looting of mail from soldiers addressed to their families—so often with money enclosed—became a scandal. So again the Post Office Department turned to lessons already learned in long experience by the British Post Office where, because of a different national temperament, the postal-money-order service had long been a success.

Between November 1, 1864, and the surrender of the Confederacy in April of 1865, only 141 post offices were equipped to issue money orders. Even so, more than 1.3 million dollars' worth of these were sold, at fees of ten cents for amounts less than twenty dollars and twenty-five cents for larger orders.

The service for soldiers, instead of dying at the end of the Civil War, boomed into big business that in its first ten years surged past the 75-million-dollar mark. This upsurge continued and during the fiscal year ending June 30, 1959, the Post Office Department issued 288 million money orders with a cash value of 5,185 million dollars.

After decades of what seemed to be a repetitious record of the United States following the lead of other countries in establishing new postal services, this country, in the midst of the Civil War, took the first bold step toward putting some order and certainty into the handling of international mails—action that led eventually to formation of the Universal Postal Union.

In the 1860's the international mail service was in a state of veritable chaos. There was no uniformity in the postal relations among different countries; the regulations governing international mail—such as did exist—were fixed by special conventions between individual governments. The result of this multiplicity of laws and regulations was intolerable confusion.

Postage rates and weight units varied not only between one country and another but within individual countries, according to the route employed and/or the zones in which the despatching and receiving offices were located. It was practically impossible for an individual to determine the best means of routing mail, and almost as difficult for government agents.

The proceeds of the postage collections were shared by the postal administrations of the countries through which consignments passed, in proportion to the value of the services supposed to have been rendered in each country. This meant that postage on every mail article had to be divided into unequal parts. It was a paradise for bureaucrats, but a sorry example of postal service. Of course the rates were very high.

What was needed, as the world's mail reached high proportions both in bulk and importance, was uniformity in rates, in security, and in handling.

Here the undivided credit for a statesmanlike outlook goes to Montgomery Blair. His organized mind was appalled at the situation and, with a rare insight into the growing need of the United States for clear channels of commercial intercourse, he decided to take steps. Oddly enough he found the need so great that his program completely skirted the traditional suspicion held by the public and the Congress for any type of foreign agreement of a permanent nature.

At Blair's suggestion, and acting through the State Department, the first International Postal Conference was convened in Paris in 1863. The delegate from the United States was John A. Kasson, First Assistant Postmaster General. Fourteen other countries sent delegates.

Wisely this convention refrained from trying to write binding agreements; its work was to determine the needs of a truly integrated postal union. It very quickly reached agreement on what was required, and on the basis of this agreement more than a score of postal conferences have been held since 1863, with each one marking a forward step in the development of security, economy, and certainty in the handling of international mail.

The substance of them all is that, based on American leadership in this instance and the fullest type of international co-operation, there simply is no question any longer about the generally expeditious and safe handling and relatively low rates of world-wide correspondence. That is, however, a continuing subject of study, just as it is a continuing service —meeting new opportunities and new problems with each new development in world politics or world transport.

Today, the Universal Postal Union, with a membership of one hundred, is one of the oldest international organizations in existence.

At this writing, the last Congress of the Union was held in Ottawa in 1957, at which suggestions for improving operations were adopted, to become effective on April 1, 1959. The next Congress of the Universal Postal Union is scheduled for Rio de Janeiro, in June of 1962.

U.S. MAIL

A pending subject is a proposal by the United States that there be an International Letter Writing Week designated in each October for the purpose of encouraging communication between individuals and consequent better understanding between peoples.

8

No One Lives at the
End of the Line

On October 1, 1896, when frost was just beginning to nip the grass in the West Virginia hills, five men saddled their horses to pioneer a venture epochal in the life of the United States. This quintet was beginning, in the area around Charles Town, the Rural Free Delivery Service.

Three of the horsemen, carrying letters and newspapers in saddlebags, rode out to the farms and crossroads stores on routes extending about twelve miles each in as many directions from Charles Town. The fourth had a twenty-mile route out of Uvilla and another a twelve-mile route out of Halltown.

The service they began, continuing unbroken through the

years since and varied only to adapt it to faster means of locomotion for the carriers, is a saga of the development of American community life. From its very beginning, this "rural Uncle Sam" has supplied a vital link in communications far beyond the formality of delivering the mail.

In the years prior to general telephone service, in particular, the rural mailman was the speedy rider who would carry news of forest fires, of accident, or an outbreak of illness on a farm, to the nearest communications center. Unofficially he (or she) became the bearer of local news, or gossip if you wish.

And, despite regulations to the contrary, many of the R.F.D. route men would begin their daily rounds as laden with chores for their customers as with stamped mail—a spool of thread urgently needed by a housewife who had run out the previous day; a box of rubber rings for preserve jars, or a pair of boots to replace those Johnny had lost while playing in the mud.

It is true that rural delivery services were growing at this time in some European countries, but the atmosphere was different. Already, in that day, the countries of western Europe were compact and crowded, usually with farms clustered around villages. Neighbors there felt, and still feel, remote if one hundred yards separate their houses; a quarter mile or more was average in the United States—too far to call out a message, and perhaps miles from the nearest town should a crippling emergency strike a household.

The institution of Rural Free Delivery Service thus came as the lifting of a curtain that both lighted and lightened the never-inconsiderable hardships of rural life in the days preceding well-paved roads and speedy means of communication. And this was fact as well as dramatic poesy because from the very first, the rural carriers worked within a pattern of tradition—"the mail must go through"—already etched on the postal records by the city route delivery men.

Most assuredly these pioneers did not take the jobs with the expectation of "getting rich quick." Each of the five carriers who started the rural service took the oath of office to perform faithfully his duties for a salary of two hundred dollars a year. Of course it was assumed that this was not full-time work, but each agreed to ride several hours a day, to face the discomforts and hazards of all kinds of weather—and occasionally banditry—for about sixty-six cents per working day.

I think it fair to observe that over the long history of the United States postal service, until in very recent years, few cases could be found where postal workers were impelled very greatly by the financial rewards of their work.

Back in 1836, when the Department was formalized as a Cabinet agency of the Government, note was made that postal workers were paid considerably less for work of comparable responsibility than those in other Departments. As a step in correcting that situation in 1836 Chief Clerks were then raised to a salary level of one thousand dollars a year. Sixty years later, at the time of the establishment of rural mail delivery service, Postmaster General Wanamaker was quoted as saying that his quarter million persons handling the country's mail earned on the average less than other Government workers doing jobs of comparable responsibility. Parenthetically this seems to warrant the observation that in our democracy, until recently, the rewards of government service often have been in inverse proportion to the public service rendered.

Nonetheless, despite the meager compensation, the rural service quickly caught both public appreciation and sufficient willing recruits. Only nine months after it was started, the Post Office report listed eighty-two routes operating out of forty-three post offices in twenty-nine different states. December, 1899, saw completion of the first country-wide rural delivery service, in Carroll County, Maryland.

What is the extent of the Rural Free Delivery Service that the public receives? The statistics are staggering. This service now reaches more than 9.1 million families numbering more than 34 million individuals.

The question often is asked how determination is made concerning the extension of rural delivery services, whether on the basis of cost to the Post Office Department, for political considerations, or for other reasons?

Prior to 1915, rural service operated roughly on the rule of thumb that it might be instituted where the business justified the cost. In the first era, prior to 1915, rural service was decided generally by postmasters on the basis of self-liquidation—in fact, it normally showed a small profit, inasmuch as postmasters were in trouble financially if expenses overrode income.

Now rural services or extension of old ones have been traditionally established on the number of families served by travel miles. Thus in 1915, when means of travel were slow and time of the carrier limited by his speed of movement, four families per mile were the criterion for giving rural free delivery service. This was unchanged until the latter part of 1953 when it was reduced to three families per mile.

Finally, in 1958, when speed and economy of motorized operations had made possible lengthening of the average route to more than fifty-one miles—when a vastly greater service was being given by about 31,500 regular rural carriers compared with more than 45,000 in 1925—the requirement was reduced to two families per mile.

Since our postal service is essentially a service for the individual—and for everyone—it is equally as important to see that no one lives "at the end of the service line" as it is to adapt new electronic and mechanical devices to the movement of the mail.

A very large proportion of those living on rural routes are

included in the revolutionary innovation of "area services" to be described later, which by August of 1960 saw more than 150 million persons in the United States receiving next-business-day delivery of mail posted within their areas prior to 5:00 P.M.

In between the time when city free delivery and rural free delivery services were started by the Post Office Department, there grew a need for two other special types of services, not spectacular in themselves but which have proved their vitality in service.

One was the postal card, and the other was special delivery service. The postal card made its debut May 1, 1873, and special delivery service was established in 1885.

There is a legend about the origin of the postal card that is probably untrue, but it persists.

It revolves around an economical young woman in San Diego who had to pay postage to write to her sweetheart, but who would not buy writing paper. She wrote her epistles in minute penmanship on the reverse side of a stamp and mailed only the stamp itself.

More factually, the Post Office Department began in 1873 to sell postal cards quite similar in appearance to those still used by the billions annually. Not long afterward, stamped envelopes were added to the supplies dispensed by post offices, and thus a whole new business of large proportions was born.

The first postal cards had imprinted upon them a replica of a one-cent stamp. The card was sold for the price of the stamp alone, and in fact its cost under the contract system then in effect was little different from that of the stamps then printed by outside contractors on a bid basis. It would be some years before the Post Office Department transferred stamp manufacture to the Government Bureau of Engraving and Printing.

The postal card soon became so popular that within a decade it was available in several sizes, and was supplemented by a score of types and sizes of ready-stamped envelopes, provided either with or without return addresses. In fact, some remarks noted in the latter part of the nineteenth century by writers about the Post Office indicate a rumble of controversy over the "competition" by the Post Office—in the field of low-cost envelopes—with private printers.

The use of both postal cards and stamped envelopes has grown through the years, but less proportionately than other types of post office business, with the development of the prestige idea by business, which includes specially designed stationery for individualized business and personal correspondence, and the evolving of the private card.

Twelve years after the first issue of postal cards, the Post Office introduced "special delivery" letter service, as we know it today.

With development of the automobile and truck, as effect following the means, the earthbound postal system rounded out its history with establishment of the parcel post system in 1913.

On January 1 of that year post offices began accepting parcels for delivery through the mails, either at the responsibility of the sender and at rates per ounce or pound far less than the other classes, or insured for the value of contents at special premium rates.

By July 1 the service was sufficiently established for the parcel post service to be enlarged to include Collect on Delivery Service.

Before leaving this summary of the development of our country's postal system during this period, there is one unique development—now outdated but still provided as a "service" —to be recorded. That is the "postal savings."

The postal savings system, whereby individuals deposit money with local post offices as with a savings bank, and receive interest on their money at lower than commercial rates but with complete safety, represented a revolutionary concept in its day.

On January 1, 1911, the system was put into effect, largely as the result of agitation started almost twenty years earlier by Postmaster General Wanamaker. It eventually made the Post Office Department one of the major "savings banks" in the United States. But the public policy behind it antedated by far either Wanamaker or the law establishing this system.

We need to remember that for many generations there were few means, except in the older and larger cities, for the wage earner with small savings to find security and interest-bearing investment for his "nest eggs." Even when their savings reached proportions large enough to finance capital investments, many Americans hesitated to speculate with their money. Commercial banks had no facilities in the nineteenth century for handling of small deposits. Only a few cities had "savings banks."

In Philadelphia the savings bank had been pioneered (you may already have guessed the inventor at mention of Philadelphia) by Benjamin Franklin. In Boston, New York and a few other Northern cities there were also savings banks. These dated, however, from a period of philanthropy, having been founded as "mutual banks" by sponsors (whose profits were restricted to the amount of interest paid to depositors), principally as a means of stabilizing their communities.

Wanamaker was one among the wealthy, public-spirited men who felt that there was a severe social lack in the fact that thrifty Americans everywhere could not have proper advantages for saving their money and earning some interest

89

on it. He conducted one national survey to prove that many Americans were hundreds of miles from savings banks; hence had no recourse in saving money except to hide it in their dwellings or turn it over without interest to trustworthy (or sometimes not so trustworthy) depositories.

The idea finally matured in a program whereby the post offices received savings deposits, paid nominal interest, and then loaned the proceeds to, or deposited them in, approved national banks at rates sufficient to offset both the interest paid to "postal savers" and the estimated cost of handling the money.

Deposits boomed for many years, finally reaching a peak of almost 3.4 billion dollars in 1947, but more recent growth of savings departments in all types of banks, as well as savings and loan associations, and the over-all Federal insurance plans for savings accounts of all kinds, have made this postal service a useless drain on personnel and resources.

The Post Office Department, in its annual report to the Congress that met in January of 1960 renewed its recommendation that the Postal Savings System—having outlived with the stagecoach its usefulness—be abolished.

PART II

PART II

9

Nor Gloom of Night Aloft

Jack Knight was only in his twenties, but among fliers he was a seasoned veteran. As a pioneer "flying mailman" in 1921, he flew the leg between North Platte, in western central Nebraska, and Omaha.

Understandably he was excited when he learned the Post Office was ready to try the first transcontinental delivery of mail involving night flying, a rare and risky undertaking for the time.

The pioneer flight started from San Francisco at 4:30 A.M. on February 22. It was routine to the point where Pilot Frank Yager arrived at North Platte at 7:48 P.M., long after dark, but with the field specially lighted by flares to welcome him.

Knight was waiting to take off immediately on his usual "leg" to Omaha, but as mechanics removed the chocks that held his plane motionless during warm-up of the engine, someone noticed that the tail skid on his plane was broken. Repairs delayed his departure until 10:44 P.M., by which time heavy cloud banks obscured the moon and stars that would have simplified his navigation. Instead, he relied on a compass and occasional glimpses of the Platte River through the scattered clouds below his flight altitude which he carefully noted as 2,200 feet.

Knight arrived at Omaha at 1:10 A.M. and was told that the remainder of the experimental trip had been canceled because of bad weather and snow between Omaha and Chicago. The pilot who had been assigned to relieve him had been sent home. But Knight decided to go on.

With only a map to guide him over territory with which he was unfamiliar, and the determination of his generation of men who "flew by the seats of their pants," he took off at 2:00 A.M. and, flying eastward, passed over Des Moines, Iowa, at 3:30, only to run into a heavy snowstorm through which he had to search out the field at Iowa City. Somehow he found it, with only enough gas for ten minutes remaining in his tank, but the field was dark. The ground crew had closed the field after being notified of the official cancellation of the flight.

A watchman heard the engine of the plane, ran into the center of the field with a red flare, and this light alone guided Knight to a landing. With the help of the watchman, Knight refueled his plane and headed for Chicago, fighting a fog over the Mississippi River. He landed at 8:30 A.M. after almost ten hours of nearly unbearable tension.

The remainder of the flight eastward was routine.

The first night flight of the mail had passed into history, and air transport of all kinds was to reap the benefit.

Airmail has become so commonplace today that we take

for granted the carriage of correspondence in a few hours across the United States, or overnight to Europe. There is little surprise in statistics that United States mail flies approximately 1,000,000 miles a day on domestic routes and more than 120,000 miles a day on American planes to foreign countries.

Today we take the mechanics—even five-hundred-mile-an-hour jet plane speeds—for granted. Yet it all has happened in a short lifetime. We have barely passed the forty-year mark since establishment of the first small airmail route, and have not yet passed at this writing the fiftieth anniversary of the first experimental airmail flight, to be observed in September of 1961.

Nevertheless, there is a certain historic quality even in that brief account because the Post Office remembers that, like so many technological revolutions in the United States, those first experimental flights were made even before motorized vehicles had been accepted in any quantity for mail service on city streets and country highways.

Thus the airmail is new in the long line of development marking three hundred years of Post Office history, but it is becoming venerable in the onrushing growth of wonders marking the twentieth century.

One wonders at times, and speculates on the basis of proven factual experiment, whether another decade may not see airmail outmoded by other communications developments to be discussed later, with airplanes carrying only parcel post and other goods.

Putting aside, however, this reasonable speculation, the story of the airmail begins at Mineola, on Long Island, on a bright and weather-perfect day in September of 1911. That was only eight years after the Wright Brothers had taken the first heavier-than-air machine off the ground at Kitty Hawk.

95

A pilot whose name has fallen out of the records placed a small bag of mail in an airplane not greatly different from the type invented by the Wright Brothers, took off from the runway of a tiny airport near Mineola, and flew into the city where he dropped bags of mail on the grounds adjacent to the Post Office.

For a week, with each new trip marked by increasing suspense as to whether time was running out on the law of averages for success, the flights were repeated—in daylight, of course (night flying was still years in the future) and in clear weather. There was sufficient nervous apprehension then in the ever-present question as to whether any airplane would make its next take-off safely, whether it would hold together in the air, or whether it would land without crashing. All went well.

As is so often the case with pioneers who little realize the importance of a first step being taken, there exists only generalized description of this epochal point in human as well as postal history. All we know is the fact of success in the experiment, and that it involved much co-ordinated planning by the small number of sportsmen pilots, the individuals who worked on airplane design, and representatives of the postal service, who had to approve and supervise the official end of the experiment.

The postal team returned to Washington and prepared a report that requested the Congress to appropriate money to launch Air Mail Service. They were turned down. But they were neither the first nor the last men with new ideas to encounter initial frustration—as I can well testify!—and the Post Office Department exhibited its historic persistence in seeking to prove that there was substance in its dream.

Without appropriations for expenses, and through what amounted to contribution of time and individual money both by postal employees and the confident prophets of the "Air

Earliest known map of the post roads of the United States. Oddly out of proportion, the drawing shows the hamlets of the thirteen colonies clustered along the coast line, bound one to the other by a single path of communication—the first post road.

Benjamin Franklin's saddlebag.

A village post office about 1825, taken from a painting by Thomas Wood. The post office, seen on the right, was an integral part of the old-time general store.

In 1827, one section of the New York City Post Office was reserved "exclusively for ladies."

This young lady is demonstrating a model of the automatic parcel-post-acceptance machine which weighs the package, computes the total postage required (including insurance), affixes postage, and returns change and receipt.

This new air-conditioned Kalamazoo, Michigan, post office, is one of approximately 4,600 postal facilities built and financed since 1953 by private capital and leased to the Post Office Department.

Railway Postal Service workers sorting the mail in 1875. *Harper's Weekly.*

Automatic letter sorting in the newly modernized Washington, D.C., Post Office. Mechanical arms move letters one at a time in front of operators who punch the appropriate key which tells the machine to which of three hundred destinations each letter is going. This machine sorts up to eighteen thousand letters an hour.

INTERIOR, ARTIST VIEW TURNKEY POST OFFICE

Ⓐ POWER AND FREE CONVEYOR MAIL
Ⓑ OPENING AREA FOR METERED MAIL
Ⓒ DUMPING PLATFORM FOR COLLECTION MAIL
Ⓓ CULLING MACHINES
Ⓔ FACING—CANCELLING MACHINES
Ⓕ CONVEYORS TO LETTER SORTERS
Ⓖ PRIMARY LETTER SORTERS
Ⓗ SECONDARY LETTER SORTERS
Ⓘ SACKING AREA LETTER MAIL
Ⓙ OUTGOING ASSEMBLY LINE
Ⓚ CONTROL TOWER
Ⓛ INCOMING PARCEL ASSEMBLY LINE
Ⓜ DUMPING PLATFORM FOR PARCELS
Ⓝ PARCEL SORTING MACHINES
Ⓞ PARCEL SACKING
Ⓟ FEED LINE OUTGOING PARCELS
Ⓠ TO THE DOCKS
Ⓡ FLAT SORTING AREA
Ⓢ HAND CANCELLING
Ⓣ HANDWORK AREA

Operation Turnkey, the world's first "fully automatic post office," scheduled to open in 1960 in Providence, R. I.

A pen drawing of one of the famed Pony Express Riders who, in 1860, answered an advertisement for "young skinny, wiry fellows not over 18. Must be expert riders, willing to risk death daily. Orphans preferred. Wages $25 a week..." Below, an early rural mail carrier in Idaho, packing an eighty-pound load.

A once-familiar sight—the overloaded mailman—soon to disappear entirely from the American scene.

Two of the newest mail-carrying devices to assist the mailman on his rounds.

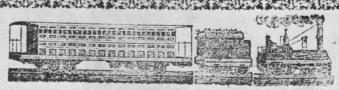

GREAT UNITED STATES MAIL LINES,

TO THE SOUTH & WEST,

VIA

BATIMORE & OHIO R. R. TO CUMBERLAND,

AND

NATIONAL ROAD TO WHEELING.

SIX DAILY LINES of Mail and Passenger Coaches
leave Cumberland every Evening, after the arrival of the
Cars at that place, for Pittsburg, Wheeling, Cincinnati,

Louisville, St. Louis and New Orleans. Through to Pittsburg or Wheeling in forty-four hours. Passengers taking
this route will be out one night only. Leaves Philadelphia
twice daily, Winter and Summer. For Seats and Through
Tickets, or entire Coaches, apply at the General Rail Road
and Stage Office, No. 45 South Third Street, or at the Rail
Road Office Eleventh and Market Streets. For Stage
Companies,

T. BLACKWELL, Agent.

N. B. The above named Offices are the only Offices that are authorized
to receipt through to Wheeling or to Pittsburg, via Baltimore.   T. B.

An 1852 advertisement showing the co-operation of stagecoaches and
railroads in hauling mail and passengers to the West.

A mail coach stopping to change horses at a relay station on the Old Boston Post Road, 1815.

The City of Providence, a side-wheeler built in Jeffersonville, Indiana, in 1880, ran the mail service from St. Louis to Natchez on the Mississippi.

PACIFIC MAIL STEAMSHIP CO.'S
Through Line
TO
CALIFORNIA, CHINA, AND JAPAN,

Touching at Mexican Ports, and carrying the United States Mail.

Steamships on Atlantic and Pacific Oceans.

ARIZONA,	COLORADO,
HENRY CHAUNCEY,	CONSTITUTION,
NEW YORK,	GOLDEN CITY,
OCEAN QUEEN,	SACRAMENTO,
CHINA,	GOLDEN AGE,
RISING STAR,	MONTANA,
ALASKA,	GREAT REPUBLIC, &c.
JAPAN,	

One of the above large and splendid Steamships will leave Pier No. 42, North River, foot of Canal Street, at 12 o'clock noon, on the 1st, 11th, and 21st of every month (except when those dates fall on Sunday, and then on the preceding Saturday), for ASPINWALL, connecting via Panama Railway with one of the Company's Steamships from Panama, for SAN FRANCISCO, touching at ACAPULCO.

Departures of the 1st and 21st connect at Panama with Steamers for SOUTH PACIFIC and CENTRAL AMERICAN PORTS. Those of the 1st touch at MANZANILLO.

Departure of 11th each month connects with the new steam line from Panama to AUSTRALIA and NEW ZEALAND. Through tickets sold.

One hundred pounds of baggage allowed to each adult. Baggage-masters accompany the baggage through, and attend to ladies and children without male protectors. Baggage received on the dock the day before sailing, from steamboats, railroads, and passengers who prefer to send down early.

An experienced surgeon on board. Medicine and attendance free.

For Passage Tickets, or further information, apply at or address the Company's TICKET OFFICE ON THE WHARF,

Foot of Canal Street, North River, New York.

Beware of all other Offices. **F. R. BABY, Agent.**

The necessity to bring California into the U.S. Mail system hastened the expansion of the ocean-going steamship lines. This poster advertised the Pacific Mail Steamship Co. in 1868.

The first mail-carrying train (above), "Adrian," in Michigan; the mail was carried in the lower compartment of the double-decker car. Below is a streetcar railway mail car in Chicago, 1912.

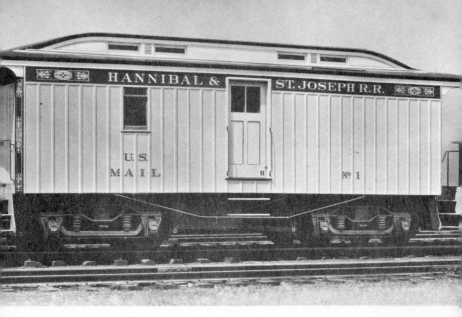

The first railway mail car which met the Pony Express at St. Joseph, Missouri.

Interior of one of the first railway post offices on the Toledo, St. Louis & Western Railway.

"Columbus in Sight of Land," after the painting by William H. Powell. On left, an Indian woman and child; on right, an Indian chief. Part of the Columbian series placed on sale in 1893.

"Fast Lake Navigation," one of a transportation series of stamps issued in 1901 to commemorate the Pan-American Exposition at Buffalo. The steamer is a side-wheeler.

In 1904, the Louisiana Purchase Commemorative Stamps were issued. This one is a portrait of Robert Livingston, U.S. Minister to France, who conducted the negotiations that resulted in the Louisiana Purchase.

Captain John Smith is pictured on the one-cent stamp issued in 1907 as part of the Jamestown Commemorative series. The painting is from an original in the Virginia State Library and the figures left and right are Pocahontas and her father, Powhatan.

A single stamp, put on sale in 1927, to commemorate the Battles of Fort Stanwix, Oriskany, Bennington, and Saratoga. It shows the surrender of General Burgoyne at Saratoga.

One of a series of twelve stamps issued in 1932 in honor of the 200th anniversary of the birth of George Washington. Taken from a miniature by Charles Wilson Peale, Metropolitan Museum.

The Maryland Tercentenary Stamp, 1934. Shown are the *Ark* and *Dove*, the two vessels on which the first Maryland colony came to America.

The Coronado Cuarto Centennial Stamp, issued in 1940 to commemorate the 400th anniversary of the Coronado Expedition through the Southwestern United States. Original by Gerald Cassidy.

The 150th anniversary of Kentucky's admission to statehood was the occasion for this 1942 stamp. Gilbert White's mural in the State Capitol at Frankfort was adapted for the design showing Daniel Boone and three companions on the banks of the Kentucky River.

The Swedish Pioneer Centennial Commemorative Stamp, 1948. The stars represent the twelve Midwestern states in which the Swedes settled in great numbers.

This special stamp in honor of Ramon Magsaysay, the late President of the Philippines, was the first to be issued in the Champion of Liberty series, inaugurated in 1957.

One of three new airmail stamps, issued in 1959 and 1960 to replace those originally issued in 1947. Each features a symbol of American liberty and a famous statement of national principle.

This Pony Express stamp was issued on the 100th anniversary of the founding of that service.

Andrew Carnegie is honored on one of the Famous Americans series, issued in New York City during 1960.

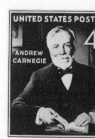

One of the first six stamps in the American Credo series, issued in 1960, which feature statements of principle by famous American leaders.

The fifty-star-flag stamp was issued July 4, 1960, in Honolulu, Hawaii, and honors the official adoption of the fifty-star flag.

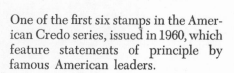

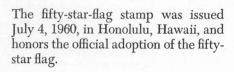

Two turn-of-the-century mail conveyances. The R. F. D. wagon (at the bottom) served the country folk of Crawfordsville, Indiana, around 1898.

A 1907 model Orient Buckboard.

A Model-T mail-delivery wagon, photographed in New York City about 1921.

A three-wheeled Wagonhal—the first government parcel-post vehicles. Tip-overs were frequent, and the chain-drive which propelled the vehicle came off at every bump. Around 1912.

A later, but still pre-World War I, development in parcel-post delivery trucks.

Among the newest devices to speed delivery of the mail is the Cushman Mailster.

The Railvan, put in operation by the Chesapeake & Ohio, in 1959, as a mail and express carrier. It has two separate sets of wheels, one to run on rails, the other on the highway.

A system of conveyors in the modernized Washington, D.C. Post Office, called "Mailflo" moves letters rapidly and efficiently between sorting areas, thereby eliminating confusion and congestion on workroom floors.

A highway post office on the road.

Interior of a modern highway post office

Readying the plane for the first regular mail flight to Philadelphia and New York from the old Polo Field, Washington, D.C., May 15, 1918.

Loading the mail for the first airmail night flight from Hadley Field New Jersey, to Chicago, July 1, 1925.

A typical airmail loading operation today.

Postmaster General Arthur E. Summerfield (3rd left), postal officials and the captain of the guided-missile submarine U.S.S. *Barbero*, Lieutenant Commander Carlos Dew, USN, watch the loading of the first missile mail.

The Regulus I training guided missile, launched from the U.S.S. *Barbero*, lands with the first official missile mail at the Naval Auxiliary Air Station, Mayport,

Postmaster General Summerfield takes the first missile-mail letters from the Regulus I.

President Eisenhower receives the first missile-mail letter from veteran Washington letter carrier Noble Upperman at the White House, June 9, 1959. Postmaster General Summerfield looks on.

A Postal Inspector checks part of the obscene material confiscated in a raid on the New York headquarters of three of the East Coast's largest dealers in pornography.

The safe arrival of the Hope Diamond, sent by ordinary registered mail to the Smithsonian Institution, was the occasion for this photograph. The gem is valued at a million dollars. (L. to R.) Postmaster General Summerfield; Mrs. Harry Winston, wife of the donor of the Hope Diamond; Dr. Leonard Carmichael, Secretary of the Smithsonian Institution; and Dr. George S. Switzer, Curator of Gems at the Smithsonian.

Postmaster General Summerfield places a wreath at the statue of the country's first Postmaster General, Benjamin Franklin, in the Ben Franklin Postal Station in Washington to honor "Postmasters' Day."

Age," experiments continued for the next five years. In state after state, city after city, wherever volunteers in aviation would give time and equipment, the airmail experiments proceeded.

Enthusiasm mounted constantly within the Department, and members of the Congress grew more impressed with what they saw. Coincidentally more and more enthusiasm for the airmail experiment was generated by the press and by community leaders.

In 1916, the Congress took the first encouraging step. The sum of fifty thousand dollars was earmarked—in an over-all appropriation for "steamboat or other powerboat" service—for the financing of an experimental airmail venture.

The Post Office Department, anxious to prove its point, immediately advertised for bids for service in two widely separated and markedly different areas—designated routes in Massachusetts and Alaska.

Frustration followed the attempt because prospective bidders discovered that while any little airplane could make the short exhibition hops that had marked prior experiments, suitable planes for operating a regular airmail service simply could not be found.

If there was to be airmail service at that time, the Government would have to turn to its own resources, which now included a fledgling air service operated as a branch of the Signal Corps by the Army.

In May of 1918, the United States was in the midst of the great build-up of military force that was to turn the tide of World War I and bring an Allied victory in the following November. Yet the tensions of this unprecedented war effort did not divert the imperative demand for progress in handling the mail.

Congress, in the spring of 1918, had appropriated one

hundred thousand dollars for inauguration of airmail service. On May 15, President Woodrow Wilson personally went to an airfield near Washington to witness the departure of the first regular airmail flight in this country's history. The plane took off for New York, from which another plane started for Washington.

This 218-mile air route served in the following year as the great experiment out of which plans and procedures could be developed. The planes were supplied by the Army and the pilots were military aviators. Not least among the experiments was the determining of costs and charges, which encountered dramatic changes before airmail was extended to other routes.

The first letters carried over the New York–Washington air lane were charged twenty-four cents an ounce, of which fourteen cents was for special postage and ten cents was a special delivery fee. Two months later the rate was cut to sixteen cents, and at the end of six months, on December 15, the special delivery service was eliminated and air postage was established at six cents for this run, or three times the then-current postage rate for regular first-class mail.

Thereafter the steps in airmail development came rapidly.

On the first anniversary of the regular initial flights, a line was started to connect Chicago and Cleveland, which later was to be a leg on the transcontinental route, and within ten weeks, despite the dangers of mountain flying over the Alleghenies, Cleveland was linked to New York, via a stop at Bellefonte, Pennsylvania.

In the following spring, airmail service flew westward from Chicago to Omaha, Nebraska, and on September 8 of the same year, the route was extended from Omaha to San Francisco. Thus transcontinental airmail service flew its first faltering legs, but it had come to stay—and to grow in a manner that probably none of the pioneers could foresee.

The planes that flew this route are today's museum pieces. They were small biplanes with engines delivering less power than the average automobile carries under its hood today. Fixed wheels served as landing gear, with a drag instead of a wheel supporting the tail. The planes had no brakes. The pilots sat in open cockpits alone, as the lift that might support a copilot represented the "pay load" of mail bags.

There was no radio communication, let alone radar or other weather helps. Landing fields literally were "cow pastures" without electric lights, controls or any other facility except gasoline.

Hence the initial transcontinental flights had to be timed for the daylight hours on each leg. Even so, the schedules maintained by the end of 1920 were twenty-two hours—almost a whole day—faster than express trains carrying the mail from coast to coast.

The Post Office Department, the pilots who flew the planes, and the growing aviation industry began to concentrate on the next great problem—what would be called in modern language "breaking the night barrier." Regular night flights would double the flying time in summer and triple it in winter, with like reduction in delivery time.

The breakthrough, with these primitive planes whose top speed seldom exceeded 125 miles an hour, came on February 22–23, 1921, when Post Office pilots relayed the mail from San Francisco to an airfield at Hazelhurst, Long Island, in thirty-three hours and twenty-one minutes. This was the venture in which Pilot Knight made his epic night flight.

At last the flying mailmen could boast full membership in the service under the old motto, "Neither rain, nor snow, nor heat, nor gloom of night stays these couriers from the swift completion of their appointed rounds."

Before the Congress then in session adjourned, it appropriated $1,250,000 for expansion of airmail service and ground facilities, the latter of which would benefit all types of aviation. What had been an isolated "stunt" now had to be placed on a stable basis.

The Post Office Department, although capable of occasional dramatic feats to prove a point, was in fact a careful and conservative operator in the air. Both in 1922 and 1923, while forging ahead with pioneering operations, it also won the Collier Trophy in each year for the most important contribution to the development of aeronautics through its safety record.

The month of July, 1924, saw airmail running on regular twenty-four-hour transcontinental service, with such a record of reliability that it was being taken for granted. The postage rate was high—twenty-four cents an ounce for the full distance—but now the difference between coast-to-coast air service and surface transportation was measured in days rather than hours.

And with the passing of the pioneering stage, the time had arrived for the Government to get out of the operating business and return to its traditional policy of giving the airmail routes to private contractors, just as it let contracts to low bidders for surface transportation. In 1926 a start was made in this direction and by August 31, 1927, every airmail route was handled by private operators.

Then attention was turned to rates, as plane capacity grew larger and cost per mile dropped. Before 1927 ended, airmail rates were reduced to ten cents per half ounce, without regard to postal zones. In 1928, the rate was reduced to five cents for the first ounce (the usual maximum rate for an individual letter) and ten cents for each additional ounce.

Since then the rates have fluctuated: down to eight cents an ounce in 1932 and to six cents in 1934; back to eight cents in World War II; then to a low of five cents in 1946, and most recently, in 1958, up to seven cents, which is less of an increase since 1946 than the increases in the cost of virtually all other services.

No nationally notable figures were on hand, but an enthusiastic crowd of descendents of Northwestern pioneers went out to wave their hats when Edward Hubbard took off from Seattle, Washington, on October 15, 1920, for Victoria, British Columbia.

We do not know whether Hubbard experienced the glow of a sense of destiny or history in the making, but on that day he wrote his name indelibly in the history of the airmail. He was the first to fly the mail on regular schedule to a foreign country, and the first private contractor employed anywhere to deliver airmail.

Equally important for the future of aviation was the contract given to Hubbard—a tangible means of supporting an aviation business rather than dependence on the helter-skelter income of gypsy flights. The Post Office contracted to pay Hubbard two hundred dollars for the completion of each round-trip flight to Victoria.

The Victoria-Seattle service, which continued without interruption until June 30, 1937, was flown over a seventy-four-mile route which, by the vagaries of geography, cut considerable time from the delivery schedule of trans-Pacific mail.

Steamers bound for the Orient on the Great Circle course across the Pacific made Seattle their last port of call on leaving the United States and their first on returning. However, for Canadian passengers and freight they made an intermediate stop at Victoria, the large island that lies off the west coast of Canada. Such stops would hold up ships from one to three days.

The object of the Hubbard service was to fly mail from the United States in time to catch outgoing steamers in the final hours before leaving Victoria, and to pick up immediately after their arrival at Victoria on the eastward passage, mail carried by them from the Orient. For business correspondence, bank drafts, and similar valuable mail the saving in time was extremely valuable.

Airplanes still had very limited ranges, and in case of accident flying over water presented hazards far greater than the land flights; but where the waters were narrow enough, the difference between plane and boat time was vital.

Before 1920 was ended, another foreign-airmail service was established between Key West, Florida, and Havana, Cuba. This service was discontinued in 1923, but it had helped to improve knowledge and techniques. In 1927, with development of the first proven seaplanes, regular airmail service to Cuba was reinstituted, and that date marks the beginning of airmail service that within a decade was extended to all of South America.

In the meantime, airplane development lunged ahead to the point where long overwater flights in still primitive but highly reliable airplanes were feasible.

By 1935 the mail was flown on regular schedule from San Francisco to the Philippines, in relays linking islands that became known to every American in 1941 through the onslaughts by the Japanese fleet. First stop out of San Francisco was Hawaii, and the others in turn were Midway, Wake, and Guam.

On April 21, 1937, the United States mail completed crossing the Pacific by extension of this route to Hong Kong—a service incidentally that tolled the death knell for the little route from Seattle to Victoria.

The first Atlantic crossing for regularly scheduled mail and passenger seaplanes or amphibians ran, in 1939, from New York, to Bermuda, to Portugal, and terminated at Marseilles, France. Another route, following more nearly the direct Great Circle course across the Atlantic, was established between New York and British airports with stops in Canada and Newfoundland.

The last "prewar" mail route began operations on December 6, 1941, the day before Pearl Harbor's destruction in the sneak Japanese attack—when a service crossing the South Atlantic over the relatively narrow waters between South America and Africa connected the terminals of Miami, Florida, and Leopoldville, in the Belgian Congo.

In the next four years no more overseas mail routes were established, as war demanded all of the resources that otherwise might have been devoted to this program. Yet out of war came accelerated aircraft development and aviation knowledge that were to outmode all prior operations and place exciting new facilities at the disposal of the postal service.

Spurred by war needs, the airplane manufacturers developed—first as bombers and then as transports—the powerful four-engine planes capable of nonstop flights with mail and passengers across continents and the Atlantic Ocean. Next came the jets, and a host of other subsidiary crafts available for special services.

In 1960 it could be stated without exaggeration that the airmail time nonstop across the United States was little more than six hours, that only eight hours separated New York and London, and that Africa and the Orient were little more than a day away.

It is impossible to estimate the value to business and to person-to-person relationships of this ability to communicate. American flagships circle the globe, and there is no spot inaccessible to the winged mail messenger that travels over the highways of the air.

Looking back on the tremendous strides that have been made, the postal service is proud of the part that it has played in fostering and developing air transport. The Post Office Department looks forward with high hope to the future of airmail as a bond of communication between the peoples of the world, an outlet for the dissemination of news and culture and exchange of thought, and a vital and real force for peace and understanding among nations.

It is not generally realized to what an extent helicopters have been used to expedite the handling of airmail between central post offices and airports, or the quantity of mail—bearing normal first-class postage—that is expedited in its travel by partial or total carriage by air when facilities permit.

Although the helicopter serves the needs of airmail, it is apart from the normal airmail operation in the sense of over-land carriage.

The "airlifts" are increasingly widespread regional operations whereby regular first-class mail is loaded aboard air-planes that have more capacity for contract mail poundage than the airmail requires at the time of flight, and this mail is moved by air to or from the major railroad distribution centers.

The two services are grouped here for brief description, but are otherwise unrelated except as dramatic examples of the forward march toward maximum efficiency in serving the public.

1. Helicopter Service

While airmail provides the speediest means yet used to send written communications, the delays in hauling airmail to and from air terminals and post offices represents loss of time that sometimes all but abolishes the advantage of air carriage.

This problem was first tackled in the late 1930's when an autogiro service was flown experimentally between Camden, New Jersey, and the roof of the General Post Office in Phila-delphia.

Later, in 1946, an experiment was conducted at Los Angeles, with helicopters operating directly from the roof of the Los Angeles Post Office. Similar tests were conducted at Chicago in the same year, and finally at New York in 1947.

The time saved was so great that in 1947 regular helicopter service was placed in operation in Los Angeles, with similar services following at Chicago in 1949 and at New York in 1952.

Actually, far more persons than the residents of these cities benefit from this service. Approximately 120 cities have much faster delivery of airmail as a result of helicopter service. This is because of the "area" system we have put into operation in recent years, under which certain large cities are "area headquarters" for the cities surrounding them. Thus the New York "area" consists not only of the city proper but many counties in New York, Connecticut, and New Jersey.

2. Airlift for First-Class Mail

Simply defined, the airlift idea is based on the use of available unused space aboard airplanes for the carriage of mail that otherwise would have to await later surface movement. It was a conception of this postal administration and has already been approved in a test case carried to the Supreme Court of the United States, after it was challenged by the Atchison, Topeka and Santa Fe Railroad.

The need for the service has become critical in many cases, as available railroad transportation has declined sharply due to curtailment of train schedules.

At this point, I wish to emphasize that the railroads still are the backbone of the postal transportation system and, though many will find the information surprising, are paid more money today for transporting mail than ever before in history. Furthermore, the Post Office Department has cooperated in every way possible to permit railroads to continue to carry the mail. Yet in the past two years alone, 386 mail-carrying trains were eliminated by the railroads because of lack of other types of business.

Actually, the Post Office and the railroads in these cases have been caught "between the devil and the deep blue sea," and our first job is to see that mail gets in and out of cities and their environs at the fastest possible rate. If trains that might carry mail run infrequently or are abandoned altogether on some routes, our job is to find replacement transportation, and this has to be either on the highways or in the air.

So we turned to a study of what might be done with available extra space on airliners, under agreements reimbursing airlines for this extra service, but at rates lower than the standard airmail contracts.

The problem that led to experiments with the airlift grew out of the very elements marking the progress of the United States: population increase, the growth of the economy, and the evolution of the national transportation problem. For the Post Office this means that the nation's post offices today handle daily, in addition to local mail, 66 million pieces of intercity first-class mail. While this pays lower rates than airmail, it always has been and is preferential mail defined by law as "a preferred service." It must be moved as quickly as possible.

For the past century this "quickly as possible" meant railroad transportation, except for specific airmail. But about twenty-five years ago the railroad map began to be altered drastically. Train service was, until the 1930's, frequent on main trunk lines and good on almost all branch and local lines. In 1920, for instance, 80 per cent of all passenger traffic between cities moved on railroads. This provided abundant trains for the mail.

By 1949, however, passenger traffic on the railroads had dropped to 8 per cent, only one tenth of the 1920 percentage;

and by 1957, due principally to the great expansion of automobile travel, the railroads retained less than 4 per cent of intercity passenger travel.

This meant discontinuance of passenger trains by the thousands, and often the passenger schedules that were preserved were convenient for travelers but inconvenient for the mail. To reach the highest point of efficiency, the Post Office has to move as much mail as possible overnight. This can be delivered the following morning. A daylight trip for the mail usually means a wasted day for the letter writer.

And while the mail trains were diminishing rapidly, the volume of mail was increasing at a rate greater than ever before. The problem was critical at the time I assumed the Postmaster General's duties in 1953. We started immediate studies. Since then we have worked out many problems, including assistance to the railroads in readjusting schedules to handle more mail, and have put large quantities on the highway via trucks and buses. But highway travel is too slow for all except relatively short distances, so we had to turn to the air.

By October, 1953, the Post Office was ready to start two experimental airlifts, on routes between New York and Chicago and between Chicago and Washington. From the start, two things were proved: (1) that the service would take a great load off the first-class mail, and (2) that the cost to the Government was no greater. We do not feel that the railroads have been penalized by loss of revenue, although arguments to the contrary have been made.

If there is some truth in this contention, it should be remembered that the public service is paramount and that the mail must be moved. On the other hand, if air transport were used to the maximum possible for first-class mail in the foreseeable future, the volume would not amount to more than one twenty-fifth of the total of non-local mail.

In 1958, the total amount of mail sent by air was less than 74,000 tons, of which 45,872 tons were regular airmail and 25,000 tons were airlift first-class.

To put the picture in dollar perspective, the airlift mail cost the Post Office Department 3.3 million dollars compared with 336 million dollars paid the railroads for mail work.

Regional development of the airlift has created honeycombs of service routes within New England and the eastern Great Lakes region; from Chicago southward to St. Louis; a southwestern network embracing the great reaches of Texas and Oklahoma and extending westward to Albuquerque, New Mexico; a northern Rocky Mountain area centering around Salt Lake City, and various north-south routes on the Pacific Coast.

In its aim to give "next morning" delivery of first-class mail, the Post Office Department has had to wrestle with the problem of how much mail could be delivered how far between the "critical hours" of midnight and 6:00 A.M., and has reduced its figures by experience to 350 miles for railroads, compared with 1,000 or more miles even for "feeder" airlines. In the same reckoning, buses could be counted upon for no more than 250 miles, trucks for 175.

It is evident that airlift was the only answer to the imperative demand for rapid delivery of first-class mail in many places.

10

Stamps—Picture Gallery of Our Glories

Closely guarded in the collections of a few philatelists are a few twenty-four-cent airmail stamps issued in 1918 in which the picture of an airplane was printed upside down. Few of these reached the public, but one sheet of this stamp was sold at Washington, D.C., to a Mr. Robey. That was all, but it has made collecting history.

A single one of these uncanceled stamps has realized over $6,000 on at least two occasions, with a corner block of four of these stamps bearing a plate number now being valued at $35,000.

In the open market for other rare stamps, one reads in catalogues about scores of other stamps that have achieved less fantastic but relatively ridiculous values: the ten-cent Washington stamp of 1847 in unused condition that now brings about $150 for a single copy, and the far more recent 1919 Victory issue of a three-cent stamp that trades for about $4.00.

As a matter of fact the values of "rare stamps" are set exclusively by the open collectors' market, and are neither fixed nor officially acknowledged by the Post Office. To us, each stamp is worth exactly its stated value as postage. Then why these astronomical quotations?

We in the Post Office do not believe that most collecting is done with the idea of profit as a primary motive: rather it is the desire to participate in an exciting game, to achieve possession of something acknowledged to be rare. Actually our stamps approach infinity in number.

More than 60 *billion* times a year, Americans mail letters, postal cards or parcels. Postage on about half of this mail is paid by means of printed cancellation, the so-called permit mail, but still the annual stamp business transacted by the postal service defies imagination. It breaks down about as follows: 28 billion adhesive postage stamps, ranging in units from one-half cent to five dollars; 2.5 billion stamped envelopes; 3 billion postal cards; and 28 million air-letter sheets.

Postage constitutes the principal postal revenues, and stamps represent the handy medium whereby we now take it for granted that a letter dropped in any U.S. mailbox will find its way to the addressee. Thus as a business alone postage stamps have become a phenomenon of the American business and social system, since, as was remarked earlier, two thirds of all the world's mail is sent and received by our relatively small segment of the world's population.

But once we have blinked at the statistics, and focused our eyes on the meaning and use of postage stamps, we see more clearly the development of a whole cultural world that has come about in little more than a century.

The postage stamps of a nation are a picture gallery of its glories. They depict in miniature its famous men and women, the great events of its history, its organizations, its industries, and its natural wonders.

Stamp collecting has become one of the world's great hobbies, attracting such well-known figures out of the past and the present as King George V of Great Britain, who developed his collections from childhood, and Francis Cardinal Spellman of New York City, who possesses one of the world's best-known collections.

Stamp collecting has distinct educational values. No one can pursue this hobby intelligently without developing a greater knowledge of his heritage.

It is the responsibility of the Post Office Department to recognize this fact, and in the past few years we have found new and great values in carrying the message of democracy both to our own people and to foreign peoples by means of our postage stamps.

Let me emphasize that no special postage stamp has ever been sold in the United States as a means of creating new postal revenue; every stamp issued by the Post Office is sold at its face value, and is worth no more or less on a piece of mail. Our responsibility has been that of deciding upon a limited number of special commemorative issues of outstanding historical interest; and this Administration established a seven-member Citizens' Stamp Advisory Committee to insure good judgment in that selection.

Stamps issued by the U.S. government may be grouped in these categories:

Regular stamps for prepayment of postage are always kept in constant supply and changed in design only at approximately fifteen- to twenty-year intervals. These descend from the first stamps issued in 1847—the ten-cent black Washington stamp and the five-cent brown Franklin stamp. Such stamps

111

still traditionally bear portraits of former Presidents, other prominent persons or national shrines without especial reference to anniversaries. As an instance, the most common stamp in use early in 1960—the four-cent stamp for first-class mail—bears a portrait of Abraham Lincoln. It was issued November 19, 1954. As a matter of precise interest this stamp and most other "regular" stamps measure 0.75 by 0.87 inches.

Commemorative stamps date from the 1893 Columbian Series issued at the time of the Chicago World's Fair. These are the stamps that we are now using in increasing volume to celebrate events and persons associated with the development and ideals of the nation and, more recently, to carry abroad the basic messages of our democracy.

Champions of Liberty stamps are really a segment of the commemorative stamp group and are used to honor foreign fighters for ideals of freedom, ranging in time and personalities from Simon Bolivar, the South American liberator, to Ernst Reuter, Mayor of Berlin, during the Soviet "blockade."

Memorial stamps are issued at rare intervals to honor an American official who dies in office. There were, among others, a two-cent memorial stamp for Warren G. Harding issued September 1, 1923, and four Franklin D. Roosevelt stamps in 1945–46.

Airmail stamps, first issued in 1918, essentially bear symbols of aviation and airmail developments. These include both "regular" and "commemorative" types.

Special stamps mark mail prepaid for special services such as special delivery, or for postage due, etc.

The total of commemorative stamps had passed the 450 mark by January of 1960, but the rate of growth of this total has been arbitrarily slowed by limiting those presently issued to about a dozen a year.

Commemorative stamps hold the modern collectors' greatest interest, and special sales of them now profit the Post Office

Department about 27 million to 30 million dollars a year because, while the stamps are sold at face value, collectors put them away and rarely use them on mail requiring service. More important, their value in highlighting the ideals of freedom is beyond measurement. Today the Post Office usually distributes 120,000,000 stamps of each four-cent commemorative issue—certainly not a limitation by scarcity.

When commemorative stamps are issued, there is still another operation, now traditional, known as the "first day of issue," from a post office designated because of its connection with the event, person or place involved. This also has become a matter of high collecting interest and consequent development by the Post Office in response to the demand.

Many readers will know well the "first day covers," which are envelopes properly addressed and stamped, with the postmark of the first post office of issue carrying the date of the "first day."

These first-day covers figure to a relatively small degree in the stories of high values attached to rare stamps. They go out of circulation and generally out of sight, as the prized possessions of individuals with direct or indirect interest in the event commemorated.

The manifestation of interest in first-day covers reached a new record proportion on February 8, 1960, when the Washington, D.C., Post Office canceled in that one day 1,419,955 letters specially filed for affixing of the four-cent Boy Scouts of America Golden Jubilee commemorative stamp. This Boy Scout stamp is one of the first examples of the traditional Post Office effort—not always conspicuously successful—to combine beauty with utility in design.

It would have been an easy matter from the start to issue postage stamps bearing simply a numeral on the face of each, showing its denomination. So why were our stamps, from the

113

very first issues, commemorative stamps in the sense that each bore the likeness of a person, and that very soon "things" were added to the subjects depicted?

One answer might be that the United States adapted the British pattern of putting a portrait of its sovereign on its stamps. But there is more to it than that; from the beginning the intricate designs of stamps have been a part of the security plan for protection against easy duplication, or counterfeiting. And, of course, there was the basic reflection of national pride.

Behind even these two factors, however, was a tradition established in the eighteenth century in the production of bank notes and, for that matter, official papers and even literature, which from the dawn of modern manuscripts had been marked by "illuminations," illustrations, and decorative devices. Man has an insatiable desire for beauty in utilitarian things, whether he often realizes it or not.

Thus it was natural that when the first United States postage stamps were issued, they should have a theme carried out in the miniature space afforded. And what was more natural than that George Washington, the Father of His Country, and Benjamin Franklin, father of the United States Post Office, should have the first places? Their portraits, enclosed within intricate frames cut by engravers of infinite patience and skill, made quick counterfeiting almost impossible.

The series of 1847 was superseded in 1851 by another issue, broadened to meet newly set rates, and comprising eight different stamps, in which Benjamin Franklin was shifted from the five-cent to thirty-cent denomination. Thomas Jefferson won a place on the five-cent stamp and the others all bore various poses of Washington. There was also a one-cent "Carrier" prepaid delivery stamp that introduced the eagle into stamp design; it was the first stamp that was wider than it was tall.

The stamps of 1847 and 1851 were invalidated after the

Civil War began, and the new series of 1861–69 saw Andrew Jackson (1863), and Abraham Lincoln (1866) joining the gallery of stamp immortals.

Thereafter for half a century the postage stamps of the United States developed into a national gallery of portraits—often busts of men modeled as Greek figures in the classical traditions that came with the Victorian days. Those with beards were almost frightening, but the engravers did their best with the material at hand, although it takes a catalogue to help identify the names behind the faces on many of the stamps.

During the period prior to 1894, postage stamps were printed and engraved by private contractors, with the National, Continental, and American Bank Note companies, as the successive contractors. In 1894 the Bureau of Engraving and Printing, established within the Treasury Department to produce United States currency, also became the official producer of stamps, as it remains to this writing.

Until only a little more than two years ago, the Bureau also designed the stamps. Then a new nongovernmental group was formed to recommend subject matter for new stamps and to bring the services of noted artists into the first steps in stamp production.

In the meantime, postage stamps had branched out into numerous specialized fields—registry, special delivery, postage due, etc. And there were odd mistakes in choice of colors, as when in 1894 the then current special delivery stamp caused confusion because of its close resemblance to the one-cent and four-cent Columbian Commemorative stamps—and accordingly was shifted to an orange color until the whole design was changed later in the year.

In 1957 we began to print multi-colored stamps on the Giori press, which can print stamps of three colors simultaneously applied. The press itself is a marvel of modern invention. Fittingly enough the first stamp produced by the Bureau of Engraving and Printing on the Giori press was an issue bearing a color rendition of the United States flag (1957).

Any attempt either to catalogue American stamps or to describe in detail their development is frustrated here by lack of space, but for stamp collectors, students and historians, the Post Office Department has produced some easily obtainable literature.

Today the Post Office Department is the recipient of many awards both at home and abroad for its recent work in stamp design. In 1959 L. Rohe Walter, Special Assistant to the Postmaster General, whose responsibilities embrace supervision of the Department's stamp program as part of our public relations work, was awarded the signal honor of being named "Philatelic Man of the Year," by the National Philatelic Museum.

The important lesson we have tried to learn and use is that stamps have a mission which, if properly appreciated, makes each one equivalent to "the picture worth ten thousand words."

What do commemorative stamps commemorate? This is a question often asked. They commemorate a wide range of events, dates and persons of interest to a large segment of Americans or of the world's population, and significantly the two fields of interest are drawing closer and closer together.

On July 19, 1960, as this book was going to press, the post offices at Sacramento, California, and St. Joseph, Missouri, opened the business day with first sales of a four-cent stamp and a stamped envelope, respectively, commemorating the one hundredth anniversary of the start of the Pony Express, and the first members of a relay of pony riders began retracing the historic route between St. Joseph and Sacramento both ways.

Only fifteen days earlier, on July 4, had been issued the first stamps bearing an American flag with fifty stars—this being the first official date of display of the new national emblem.

In this same year of 1960, other new stamps covered such different fields as the fiftieth anniversary of the Boy Scouts of America, the Olympic Winter Games, the Boys' Clubs of America, the SEATO Conference, Water Conservation, and the Fifth World Forestry Congress.

In a separate and special category are a series of six "American Credo" stamps with quotations from George Washington, Thomas Jefferson, Benjamin Franklin, Patrick Henry, Francis Scott Key, and Abraham Lincoln.

The American Credo stamps, all of four-cent denomination, each represent—repeated 120 million times over—famous sayings that are our treasured words of freedom. I think they are worth perpetuating here as instances of the message service— daily reminders to us all—that stamps can carry:

WASHINGTON—Observe good faith and justice toward all nations.

JEFFERSON —I have sworn . . . Hostility against every form of Tyranny over the mind of man.

FRANKLIN —Fear to do ill, and you need fear Nought else.

HENRY —Give me *liberty* or give me *death*.

KEY —And this be our Motto, in God is our Trust.

LINCOLN —Those who Deny freedom to others Deserve it not for Themselves.

The introduction of the George Washington credo stamp appropriately took place at Mount Vernon, Virginia, from which "first-day covers" were mailed. This stamp, devoid of any personal portrait, is a particularly beautiful example of design work, with the quotation supplemented by a pair of scales and a reproduction of Washington's signature.

The story behind this stamp, and the five others following it in the series, illustrates many factors in the underlying philosophy of our program to make stamps another major element in the telling of the American story. The lives of those who first bespoke the ideals of our nation lie behind us, but their words expressed in the timeless credos live today, and no stamp series has received wider or warmer appreciation. This has amply justified the effort behind them.

Late in 1957 the Post Office Department's Citizens' Stamp Advisory Committee began consideration of this series. One hundred Americans prominent in public life and education were asked to state opinions on the project. We sent to them twenty-four suggested "credo" quotations and asked for an evaluation of the relative importance of each.

The Washington quotation won almost unanimous endorsement as the first and major one. It is taken from his Farewell Address, delivered September 17, 1796.

Three major steps are involved in the selection of each commemorative stamp, all designed to make the most of the inspirational messages they bear—a factor that more and more is guiding even the periodic new issues of unlimited "regular stamps."

First, there is the selection of topic; second, the design, color and message; and third, the news generated by issuance of the stamp.

In March of 1957 we established the Citizens' Stamp Advisory Committee, "to advise the Post Office Department on subject matter, design, production, and issuance of postage stamps with the most appropriate and appealing themes." It has since worked with the Special Assistant to the Postmaster General, Mr. Walter, serving as the Department's liaison.

The Committee membership includes William H. Buckley,

118

of the Art Directors Club of New York; Arnold J. Copeland, of the Westport [Connecticut] Artists Association; Bernard Davis, Director of the National Philatelic Museum; Sol Glass, president of the Bureau Issues Association; H. L. Lindquist, chairman of the National Federation of Stamp Clubs; Ervine Metzl, of the Society of Illustrators; and Abbott Washburn, Deputy Director of the United States Information Agency. There has been only one replacement. Franklin R. Bruns, Jr., who was Curator of Philately and Postal History, of the Smithsonian Institution, was named Director of the Post Office Department's Division of Philately. Bernard Davis took his place.

Working as ex-officio members of the committee are the government officials who must produce and publicize the stamps, so that there is, in the chain of decision, no hitch between the ideas produced by the advisory committee and the practical matters faced by the men who must produce the stamps.

I would like to emphasize also the significance of the inclusion of an official of the USIA on this committee because we consider the impact of certain issues of stamps on our friends in other parts of the world to be of the highest importance.

How does this system work? Here is an example:

The fiftieth anniversary of the founding of the Boy Scouts of America came on February 8, 1960. This is a "natural" in anniversaries, beyond dispute as to appropriateness, and plans were laid long in advance for the issuance of the stamp. In this case, the committee was chiefly concerned with the production of an appropriate stamp. It went over the long list of artist-designers who co-operate with the committee, and who, for much less than their commercial rates, design these stamps. The natural selection, unanimously agreed to, was Norman Rockwell, whose covers for *The Saturday Evening Post* and *Boy's Life*, the Boy Scout magazine, have been noted for a score or more of years as peculiarly indicative of the American

119

and Scout scenes. Rockwell accepted the assignment and submitted a design, which was approved.

From the inception of the idea until the stamp was produced, under the system now in effect, there has been a continuity of understanding, backed by an assurance of appropriate design and taste.

This stamp, in fact, marked Rockwell's debut as a "stamp artist," and he has indicated that he felt as honored at being chosen as the Post Office was to have his talents. Other outstanding illustrators who have recently designed stamps include Denver Gillen, Bradbury Thompson, Frank Conley, Homer Hill, Rene Clark, Rudolf Wendelin, Richard Lockwood, Robert Hallock, Stevan Dohanos, George Samerjan, Robert Baker, Austin Briggs, Joseph Feher, Walter Hortens, Suren Ermoyan, Robert Foster, Charles H. Carter, Herb Lubalin and Harold Von Schmidt.

Frank Conley is the first of the illustrators to have the distinction of designing six stamps simultaneously—the American Credo series. At the other extreme, artists often have cooperated on stamps of a special character involving particular problems. One such instance was the "Champion of Liberty" concept which represented the combined work of Arnold Copeland, Ervine Metzl, and William H. Buckley.

The story behind the Champion of Liberty stamps is a dramatic one. Our own people in the Post Office Department set out in 1957 to see what could be done in co-operation with the United States Information Agency to utilize postage stamps that would bear the message of American thought to foreign lands in simple and understandable terms. We know that postage stamps reach many persons cut off from the normal free press to which we are accustomed, and many other millions who seldom read newspapers or periodicals, or listen to the radio, even if these are available. But the most remote receiver of a letter usually looks at a foreign stamp and studies it. So was born the idea of the Champion of Liberty series, honoring men whose names generally have become known around the world.

In the two-year period prior to the issuance of the Reuter stamp, four other "champions" had been honored—Ramon Magsaysay, late President of the Philippines; Simon Bolivar, already mentioned; Lajos Kossuth, of Hungary, and José San Martin, of Argentina.

On the basis of first-day sales, each of the stamps was a "smash hit" from the start, and exemplified the wisdom of their selection. Furthermore, each was issued (excepting an eight-cent stamp only for Magsaysay) in the two most common denominations of their time—four-cent and eight-cent, the postage respectively of domestic and foreign regular first-class mail, with the advantage that even on foreign mail two four-cent stamps made the exact postage.

In each case, issuance of the stamps was tied to special announcement in the country and continent of the honored figure, and official ceremonies highlighting the occasions. The results were phenomenal:

The Magsaysay stamp, issued in 1957, enjoyed a first-day-cover sale of 334,558 in a year when the best sales ranged between 350,000 and 475,000 even though Magsaysay was relatively little known except in the Philippines and the United States.

The Bolivar stamp first-day-cover sales went to 708,777; the Kossuth to 722,188, the San Martin to 910,208, and the Reuter crossed the million mark. This is a veritable rain of letters, carrying to peoples throughout the world the American tribute to leaders of freedom.

The American Credo series, issued exclusively in the four-cent denomination, are more in the nature of reminders to Americans of their heritage, but since a great many letter writers buy only the standard four-cent letter stamp, and use multiples of it for their foreign correspondence, the "credos" may be fairly assumed to have gone far and wide around the earth.

We are now working on another facet of this same kind of program with the "People to People" project. At this time these plans have not matured. But it is evident that whatever course our Government takes in its domestic affairs for many years to come, the international stamp program is here to stay.

Today airmail postage, both commemorative and regular, represents a whole division of philatelic opportunity in itself.

The letter rates for international airmail divide into three categories—ten cents for Latin American countries except Mexico, where the rate is the same as for the United States and Canada; fifteen cents for European countries and a small part of northern Africa, and twenty-five cents for the remainder of Africa, Asia, Australia, and New Zealand.

In 1959, the Post Office decided to use this airmail postage in the same manner as commemorative stamps, to carry special messages abroad, but without the normal limitation on quantities as in the case of special issues.

Working with the USIA and the State Department, a series of three new denominations was devised, of which the first (the fifteen-cent foreign airmail stamp) was issued in November of 1959, the others during 1960.

The fifteen-cent stamp, which will be used on billions of letters to both the free countries and those behind the Iron Curtain in Europe, bears a symbol originating in Europe and known everywhere, the Statue of Liberty. Its simple legend is "Liberty for All."

The ten-cent stamp is somewhat similar in theme, but bears the Liberty Bell, a symbol known to every child in Latin America, where our history is intertwined with the "liberating" revolutionaries, who usually rallied their followers by the ringing of church bells. Here the inscription is "Let Freedom Ring."

For the twenty-five-cent stamp, there existed a special problem, as not too many Africans or Asiatics recognize the symbolism of either the Statue of Liberty or of the Liberty Bell. For them the message needed to be personalized, and careful surveys were made to decide the best design for a stamp. Out of these studies came the unqualified report that of all Americans notable in history Abraham Lincoln is the best known and most easily recognized in Asia and Africa. Thus it is Lincoln's likeness—already crowding George Washington in the record race for imprinting on domestic regular and commemorative stamps—that will bear airmail to three vast areas, with the homely message, *"Of the People, by the People, and for the People."*

One wonders in how many remote villages whose names may never figure in history the receipt of a letter with this stamp bearing its picture of the sad, bearded man will leave an imprint, especially on the minds of children. These peoples may never be particularly impressed by our economic statistics, but they will remember inspiring words that translate into other languages and dialects as fluently as they are rendered in our own.

The first day of issue of a new stamp—commemorative or regular—has been compared to the opening of a new show, because so many precise factors are involved. And it is well worth the trouble, since the "opening" involves a point of public interest for anywhere from 300,000 to more than 1,000,000 individuals.

When that many Americans voluntarily participate in an event it becomes worth both time and trouble, but with practice the Post Office Department has reduced both the time and the trouble to a minimum and avoided all extra cost to the taxpayers. The time of a dozen or so special employees is small payment on the part of the Post Office Department for the revenue of $40,000 (obtained from sales of a million and more four-cent stamps on first-day covers) that otherwise would never come into the postal revenue. But even if this were a deficit item in our budget, it would yield returns in public service far beyond any money cost. Happily it shows a profit.

But why, it will be asked, do we have "first-day covers" and what do they mean? Their meaning is symbolic and of great significance to those who go to the trouble to obtain them.

A good homely example is the Dr. Ephraim McDowell four-cent commemorative stamp first issued on December 3, 1959, at Danville, Kentucky. This maroon stamp meant many things to many persons, as was shown by the manner of its selection, for inclusion in the "Famous American" series.

There were three reasons for selecting this stamp and Danville as its place of introduction. First: Dr. McDowell was nominated by the Kentucky Medical Association on the basis of his fame as one of the America's great pioneer surgeons. Virginia-born, in 1771, Dr. McDowell studied in Edinburgh, and returned to the United States to set up practice in Danville, Kentucky. There, despite distance from the Eastern centers, Dr. McDowell became world famous after he perfected in 1809—150 years prior to this celebration—the technique that enabled him to perform the first planned ovariotomy. And he practiced in Danville until his death in 1830.

The American Pharmaceutical Association endorsed this nomination because Dr. McDowell, like many practitioners of his period, also dispensed his own prescriptions from a pharmacy that was a part of his residence, gaining a reputation as one of the foremost pharmacists of his age. Finally the Kentucky Historical Society recalled that Danville was the site of the first United States Post Office west of the Allegheny Mountains. Thus three items of American historical interest were joined in the issuance of one stamp and the consequent plan to make Danville the "first-day issue" post office.

Several days before the set date a specialist moved into Danville to assist the local postal force. Helping the local postal group was a temporary staff trained to fill first-day orders, particularly in the quick but precise affixing of stamps and legible canceling of the envelopes.

Awaiting the supervisor were thousands of requests sent to Danville, enclosing self-addressed envelopes and fees for the postage to be attached to them. Numerous packets of these came from dealers who specialize in handling first-day-cover orders, but great numbers were from individuals who watch for Post Office Department advance notices of these events and send in their own individual orders.

There was a special cancellation die provided by the Post Office Department, as is usual for these ceremonies. The cancellation mark harmonized with the stamp. Thus when the stamp bearing Dr. McDowell's likeness was canceled, the postal mark on the envelope showed the usual circle with hour, date and city common to all cancellations, but standing well to the left of the stamp. In the intervening space appeared a line drawing of Dr. McDowell's house and apothecary shop, while printed between the lines that overlaid and canceled the stamp were the words, "First Day of Issue."

This whole procedure and mechanical process was typical of the care given to such events.

I think that these first-day-cover sales are perhaps the most eloquent answer to the question as to whether stamp collecting in its various phases is a fad or a part of the American tradition. Many of the covers are ordered by nonrepeaters, or persons whose interest is confined to having a souvenir of one stamp mailed on its first day of issue. And some trouble and time, as well as expense, is involved in sending the proper letter and money and return envelope to complete the transaction.

Yet in the Post Office fiscal year ended on June 30, 1959—the last for which complete records were available at this writing—the twenty-nine post offices that issued first editions of regular or commemorative stamps, sold 24,427,380 stamps that were affixed to 9,742,418 envelopes. The average order for first-day covers of the twenty-three commemorative stamps included in the total of twenty-nine issues was 387,000, compared with an average of 349,562 in the prior year, which represents a remarkable growth in interest in only one year.

Yet formidable as these statistics on first-day covers appear to be, they represent only a small fraction of the Post Office's philatelic business, which has grown to such proportions that day in and day out it is a large operation in itself and one that is a matter of regular news interest shown by some seventeen hundred newspapers, many of which run regular "stamp columns."

Our philatelic work in the Post Office Department is what might be called in normal business the "new merchandise" work. We neither buy nor sell old stamps and, as was emphasized before, have no official interest in the collectors' prices.

The philatelic business of the Post Office revolves primarily around a section of offices in the Post Office Department, with some eighty "windows" located in the larger metropolitan post offices. Orders are filled either through the windows of the branches or by mail to Washington. If a collector lives near a larger center, he may buy the desired stamps, just as he purchases regular stamps for use as postage, which is the manner in which the great bulk of the philatelic business is conducted.

However, there has been a phenomenal growth in the mail-order business for what is legally termed "stamped paper," sold by mail from Washington.

Here, the philatelic agency has the same issues of stamps currently available at the branches, with a more complete stock of back issues. However, in view of the large investments made by collectors, and the trouble taken to place special orders, we make a particular effort to be sure that the philatelic purchasers obtain only those stamps with the best possible impressions, and to fill with extreme care, insofar as possible, the precise orders, which often come in large and varied forms.

The simplest of steps is involved in becoming a customer of the Philatelic Sales Agency—simply a letter of inquiry, addressed to the agency in care of Post Office Department, Washington 25, D.C., and accompanied by a stamped return envelope. Such a request will result in the return of a sheet listing all available commemorative and regular stamps and other special items such as postal cards and stamped envelopes with their prices and the instructions and costs for filling orders. Postage charges are added to the sum of money to be sent in payment for the stamps ordered.

There is a flat charge of fifty cents for registration on each order, regardless of value, where this protection is desired.

Postage rates for the return of stamp orders range from five cents for lots of one to forty-nine stamps, up to five dollars for orders of thirty-five hundred stamps or more. All the other details are given in the information form.

Thousands regularly visit the Philatelic Exhibition Room (1315) in the Post Office Department Building in Washington, and our recently opened Postal History Museum Room (1412–16).

In all, we have taken great interest and pleasure in recent

127

years in developing the usefulness of our stamps beyond their primary function in payment of postage. I believe a pattern has been set that in the years ahead will contribute increasingly to the better understanding of America's ideals both at home and abroad.

11

The War That Never Ends— the Postal Inspection Service

There comes to my desk each Friday evening from the Chief Postal Inspector a condensed report that holds the potential for mystery stories as gripping, and sometimes as horrible, as the most imaginative whodunits on the bookracks.

A crew of skilled investigators is sifting the burned fragments of a crashed airplane for evidence of a bomb explosion in its mail cargo. . . . A promoter of false stocks is arrested for victimizing hundreds of gullible persons of their life savings through false brochures. . . . A lonely hearts club, just broken up, has served as a clearing house for a nationwide prostitution operation. . . . In Los Angeles, evidence has finally been obtained to indict a dealer in unbelievably obscene pictures sold by mail to adolescents. . . . A ring of buyers for stolen stamps mounting into millions of dollars' worth has been smashed. . . . Another multimillion-dollar business in purveying fake reducing machines and exercises by mail has been smashed.

These are random samples of the daily chores of the oldest and one of the finest investigating organizations serving the American public—the Postal Inspection Service. The Inspection Service wages a constant war on many fronts against types of crime that never can be stopped by its work alone, but must be checked.

It has a multiple charge—the protection of the mails, postal funds and property; the apprehension of those who commit offenses against the postal service, and the investigation throughout the postal establishment of conditions which might affect the integrity and dependability of the service.

The Inspection Service sometimes works under handicaps because even though it may have every reason to believe that the sanctity of the seal is being used to shield unlawful communication, the protection of that seal against intrusion by anyone other than the sender and addressee closes sealed communications against examination.

The Inspection Service, in the apprehension of criminals, historically begins investigation only after the guilty have used the mails at least once, and too often this one time is sufficient for the crooked, the perverted, or the insane to do their harm. Then only relentless prosecution can be used as a tool to warn others against effective repetition of their crimes.

Unfortunately in too many cases, particularly involving vice, the Inspection Service has been hampered over the years by lax laws and penalties, or disinterest by the courts in "making the punishment fit the crime."

The Postal Inspection Service, headed since 1953 by Chief

Postal Inspector D. H. Stephens, has one of the highest rates of successful prosecutions on record. I feel free to say what this service, acting directly under the office of the Postmaster General, cannot say:—that is, that it to me is absurd to see the occasionally unfaithful postal clerk sentenced to five years in prison for pilfering the mail, while in another court the known purveyor of half a million dollars' worth of filthy pictures and, far worse, implements of sex degeneracy to minors, is fined a few hundred dollars under misdemeanor statutes.

Our Postal Inspection Service has relatively little trouble with seasoned criminals who know that, if they rob the mails, or cause death by such robberies, they have a 95 per cent chance of being caught and severely punished under Federal laws.

The greater trouble comes from the "borderline" operators of mail frauds and the purveyors of obscenity because, while convictions are obtained in the great per cent of cases that can be prosecuted, evidence and witnesses are extremely difficult to obtain and juries and courts tend to be lenient.

The result of this situation can be summed up in a single conclusion: The mails were never safer from outright burglary or tampering, but efforts to use the postal service for fraudulent and obscene activities are constantly increasing.

Both of these topics will be amplified a little later. First, however, let us look at what I consider the "Government's finest" investigating service, whose skills must cover all the fields required to protect and police the largest business enterprise in the world, and one with the peculiar features of public trust that I have tried to emphasize.

The Inspection Service is not large—for instance, in New York State there are only seventy-five Postal Inspectors—but it is a corps of specialists, composed almost without exception of men trained within its own ranks and with prior experience in the postal service itself. For instance, Chief Inspector Stephens

131

had many other types of postal experience before becoming an Inspector. For that matter, men like Benjamin Franklin, the first of the "Inspectors," whose title was "Surveyor," brought a score of talents to his forty-year postal career.

To start even a thumbnail sketch of the Inspection Service, which was old long before the Treasury's Secret Service or the Federal Bureau of Investigation were born, is to start actually with Franklin.

When Franklin was appointed by the British Government to the post of "Surveyor" of the Colonial Postal Service of North America in 1737, his duties were various and manifold: to visit post offices and bring postmasters to account, to watch against fraudulent use of or tampering with the mail, to recommend sites for new post offices and to study means of improving services. All of these remain the duties of today's Inspection Service, altered in detail more than in fact.

In later years, after the Post Office had been established under an independent government, Noah Webster was a postal inspector, as the title has been changed to read. One of his early assignments was to apprehend highwaymen who were robbing the mails between New York and Hartford, Connecticut—a fairly tempting crime in the days of mail transport by coach or lone horsemen over lonely roads and remote trails.

The Inspection Service must be the guardian of the faith under which American citizens entrust their most intimate secrets and most valuable possessions to the mails. This trust is based first of all upon the demonstrated integrity and devotion of the overwhelming majority of the more than half a million postal workers. But the service must be protected from every threat without or within.

To the postal inspector there is neither friend nor enemy in the cases he is assigned to investigate; he is charged equally with protecting the innocent from false charges and apprehending the guilty. There is no moral statute of limitations on crimes against the mails, and no cases are closed as "unsolved."

Postal inspectors enter only criminal cases which involve the mails, but once they do participate, the record shows a very high percentage of cases solved by them after other police agencies have failed. Gerald Chapman, one of the most notorious criminals ever hanged—robber, murderer and about everything else—finally was brought to ultimate justice for a postal crime.

Not all wanted criminals are caught, but unsolved cases never are closed. We still distribute a poster, dating from 1924, for a wanted criminal whose death or whereabouts has not been established.

The penalties for violations of the sanctity of the mail are stiff: up to five years' imprisonment and a two-thousand-dollar fine for stealing from the mail, whether done by one inside or outside of the postal service; the same prison sentence and a one-thousand-dollar fine for breaking and entering a post office, and (most important) a *mandatory* twenty-five-year penitentiary sentence for holding up a mail custodian whose life is jeopardized by use of a dangerous weapon.

The Postal Inspection Service is organized into fifteen divisions embracing the fifty states and the territories, with inspectors located in four hundred cities. The Service employs the most modern methods for detecting crime and has laboratories for analyzing clues; beyond that, the relative stability and length of service of the inspectors imparts a priceless fund of know-how in every field, from tracking down criminals to smelling out clues that crop up when missing but wanted suspects pop up in the reports of local police for quite different offenses. The day and night throb of teletypes connecting its far-flung field offices with the Chief Inspector writes the daily story of hundreds of fast-moving activities.

While the criminal investigation work of the Inspection

Service is of headline interest, the service operates on two broad fronts, in which its members must have equal facility, but in neither case is it a prosecutor or maker of decisions.

If the job deals with postal-service changes or improvements, it is reported to the Postmaster General, who makes the decision. If the work is in the criminal field, evidence is turned over to the United States District Attorney in the district concerned, and he decides whether a criminal prosecution is warranted.

On the service end, the inspectors analyze and appraise operations to recommend improvements, and gather technical data on possible new methods. At least once a year postal inspectors audit the books and check operations in every single post office. A Division of Internal Audit, which was organized by this administration, and assigned to the Bureau of the Chief Postal Inspector, accomplishes continuous, professional audits of all major financial activities within the Department and in the field. If discrepancies or poor methods are found, they so report. Inspectors investigate charges and complaints against postmasters and other employees. They check individuals scheduled to be nominated to key posts, act as advisers to postmasters and install and instruct newly appointed ones.

They inspect annually lands and buildings owned or leased by the Post Office Department and report on the values or limitations of property under consideration for use. In this, the Inspection Service is a vital business arm of government.

The criminal investigation work seems simple in summary, but is as wide as the country in activities. Investigations involve embezzlement and illegal withholding of funds, theft and rifling of mail, forgery and passing of money orders and postal savings certificates, mailing of bombs and other explosives, or of poisons, poison-pen letters, obscene material, extortion letters, and other illegal matter. Every case yields recommendations for improving the inspection service.

Sometimes the Inspectors are asked to co-operate with local authorities in cases that, although connected with the mail, are tried in state courts. In all cases, there is reciprocal co-operation with law-enforcement offices whether Federal, state, county or municipal. The man who robs a local post office is just as likely to rob a bank.

With numerous other investigative duties to perform inspectors can devote only 45 to 50 per cent of their time to strictly criminal violations; nevertheless 5,968 arrests for mail theft alone were made in 1959. Total arrests were 8,859, the highest in history. As an indication of the thoroughness of the investigations and adequacy of evidence presented, statistics show that 98.6 per cent of those arrested and brought to trial were convicted. A substantial part of the losses was recovered.

Inspectors find that postal people who commit major violations are but a minute fraction of the half million loyal and devoted members of the postal family. Significantly, inspectors themselves are the most outspoken in pointing out the small per cent of crimes committed by postal employees. Of 520,000 postal employees over recent years, 621 were arrested for depredations of the mail, only 170 for embezzlement of funds; truly a fine record, perhaps the best of any similar establishment in the world.

Prior to World War II, the Bureau of the Chief Inspector was assigned to work out with the War Department comprehensive plans for the handling of military mails in times of peace and war. The plans were suddenly and realistically implemented following Pearl Harbor, and postal inspectors as reserve military officers activated military postal services practically around the world. Today, a recently revised, formal agreement, executed between the Secretary of Defense and

135

the Postmaster General defining in detail the responsibilities of each department, is in effect and is co-ordinated for the Post Office by the Chief Inspector.

The position of postal inspector involves the highest type of investigative endeavor, demanding complete integrity, and the ability to determine absolutely reliable findings. The position is one of unusual responsibility requiring after special training a thorough basic knowledge of the entire Postal Service, with specialization in several important areas.

The Inspection Service provides interesting careers and exceptional opportunities for advancement and outstanding public service. Many inspectors have won enviable reputations for accomplishment and have attained high positions in the Government or in outside activities.

Unlike most employees of the Federal Government, Postal Inspectors have no fixed hours of duty. They have no time clock by which to work. If the job requires twenty-four hours of work a day they work twenty-four hours.

Since inspectors must deal with all types of emergencies such as floods, tornadoes, train and plane wrecks, they are in a duty status subject to call at all times.

12

The Menace of Mail-Order Obscenity

"Is there anything that can be done about literature like the enclosed? It was addressed to my ten-year-old girl. This is a mother's plea to do all in your power to stop this filth from coming into our home."

The enclosed "literature" to which this mother referred was a catalogue of lewd pictures accompanied by filthy comments and an appeal to the addressee—a ten-year-old child—to "break your piggy bank" and send for the merchandise offered.

Unusual? Simply the freakish work of some unbalanced degenerate? Unfortunately, no. Mail-order obscenity is a racket of serious proportions. There are no more determined, unprincipled criminals in existence than those exploiting this racket.

Their overriding goal is to extend a vast market for their filth among the children of America.

The Post Office Department is receiving complaints of obscenity in the mails at the rate of seventy thousand a year; in large part, they are coming from aroused parents such as the mother quoted above. In the most recent full year of record, our postal inspectors carried out more than fourteen thousand separate investigations, of which some ten thousand were based on complaints sent by parents.

During the year 315 arrests were made, as compared with 293 in the prior year, which in turn was 45 per cent above the previous twelve months.

The obscenity problem is one of the most difficult with which the Department has to deal, and there has doubtless been a temptation over the years to handle it as something of a "hot potato," to be discussed only in the privacy of the closed office and to be pursued quietly without disturbing the public.

As far back as 1865, Congress enacted legislation making it a Federal offense to mail matter of an obscene nature, and charging the Postmaster General with responsibility for carrying out the law. An expanded version of this basic law was embodied in the Great Postal Reorganization and Codification Act of 1872. Again in 1873 the legislation was strengthened by passage of the Comstock Act. Anthony Comstock, with whose name the law was associated, was a postal inspector whose work contributed to its enactment.

The records show many instances of diligent efforts by postal officials to keep the mails clear of indecent material. But their efforts were no more than partially successful at best. The reasons principally were that the penalties for violation of the obscenity laws were inadequate to deter persistent operators; enforcement by the courts was lax, and a largely uninformed public was making no demand either for better legislation or better enforcement.

Particularly in Los Angeles and New York, until quite recently, liberal court rulings over a period of time established virtual sanctuaries from which dealers in obscenity operated with impunity and in defiance of justice.

In the years after World War II, commercialized pornography began to expand rapidly. Under the existing laws and their interpretation and enforcement there seemed no way to check it, however intense the policing effort might be.

It was appalling to learn from a study in 1958 that the traffic in mail-order obscenity was *doubling* every five years, and had reached an annual sales "take" for the filth merchants of *half a billion dollars* a year! But even more alarming to me and to our whole postal family was the indication that the smut racketeers were concentrating on children—that, in fact, one million children a year were receiving pornographic filth in the family mailbox.

The determination was made to do everything possible to bring this heinous racket under all-out attack, including a program to inform the public fully of its existence and to help mobilize public opinion and action against it.

On the very day you may read this work, thousands of first-class (and therefore inviolable) envelopes are being dumped into the mails by filth merchants for delivery to homes, addressed to teenagers and even to younger children.

Some of this is lewd material that children have ordered and paid for. In the vastly larger percentage of cases, however, it has not been ordered at all. It arrives without the child's advance knowledge or consent.

It is sales solicitation material which, in itself, is usually debauched and rankly obscene. It goes to children—boys and girls as young as eight—without regard to their economic or

139

social or geographic status. They receive it because their names appear on a mailing list in the racketeer's hands.

Mailed obscenity generally falls into four categories:

First, and probably the foulest, are action movies depicting activities of the most depraved type imaginable.

The second category is comprised of photographs portraying acts of the vilest kinds.

The third includes pamphlets, magazines and books which describe in animalistic detail every type of perversion.

Fourth—the most troublesome, and potentially the most serious—is that commonly described as borderline obscenity, which includes nude photos, so-called art studies, and lewd advertising designed to bait purchasers into buying more degrading material.

Thus, it is not surprising that we receive thousands of letters such as these:

> The enclosed are only two of a series of most unwelcome advertising, which has been sent to my minor son over a period of years. The advertising matter has ranged from the basest of obscene literature to bargains in contraceptives. My son is now sixteen years old. His name has been on many lists dealing with coin collecting. I assume this is where these unsavory people came by it. . . .

> I am a girl of sixteen. A few weeks ago I received this in the mail. I don't want to be considered a "prude" or anything, but I consider this obscene literature, and I don't think it should be sent to girls my age. I do hope action will be taken to cease this. Thank you. . . .

For these letter writers we are devoutly thankful. They are our helpers in a task in which only the Postal Inspection Service can stand between the criminal purveyors and the public. But how few are seventy thousand complaints received in a year, representing the whole field of obscene mail! Our raids have netted single concerns with mailing lists ranging as high as one hundred thousand to two hundred thousand names! We have found a single dealer in pornography operating under 300 different names and mailing simultaneously from fifty post offices!

As an example, and an indication of the laxness of the past, let us look at one Roth who in thirty years, beginning in 1928, built up a business in pornography that was only stopped in 1959 when the aging merchant of filth was sent to Federal penitentiary for five years and fined five thousand dollars—a conviction finally upheld when it was appealed to the Supreme Court.

Roth's trial was marked by appearance on his behalf of three medical "experts" who said that they saw nothing degrading in his publications, particularly "The Aphrodite," around which the final case centered. But Roth's history as written by the Inspection Service told a different story.

He had operated under sixty-two business names, and his companies had been hit by six "fraud orders," nine "fictitious orders" and eleven "unlawful orders," but each order necessarily could affect only the company named—not Roth or his wife, who also was his partner in business, across the board. Throughout his career he had served only one three-year sentence, imposed in 1936, and otherwise had got off with numerous fines or suspended sentences. In the meantime, the Roth file had mounted to some five thousand complaints filed with the Department by Congressmen, parents, school officials, and the clergy, principally because of his contribution to juvenile delinquency.

In 1952, just prior to the time this postal administration took office, Roth was reaching a high point of business in which he purchased at the New York Post Office alone metered postage totaling $32,930.

An aroused United States Attorney in New York studied our

evidence, took up this case, obtained indictment, and pursued the case to a trial that opened in January of 1956.

From our standpoint, the decision was almost historic in its way; so difficult had it been to obtain adequate penalties in these cases either in New York or in Los Angeles, where the smut merchants largely operate.

A more recent example, and a precedent which encourages the Inspection Service, came at the end of 1959 in New York —the Encore Press case. Here a man and his woman partner were put on trial for purveying through the mails obscene movies, slides, and still photographs. After long and arduous preparation of the case, it was proved that this couple was netting some twenty thousand dollars a month profits from their relatively small operation.

Among more recent convictions, a trio in New York who pleaded guilty to a charge of mailing obscene books was fined a total of $17,500, and a California husband and wife were sentenced to five and three years imprisonment respectively for trafficking in pornography.

This trend toward stiffer sentences for distributors of obscene materials to children is heartening to all decent-minded citizens. It indicates, in my judgment, an increasing awareness by the courts of the relationship of the commercialized spread of obscenity to the increase in juvenile delinquency and other crimes, as well as an aroused public support of the crusade to clean up the mails.

Public officials close to the problem believe there is a direct connection between the fact that the percentage of rapists under twenty has doubled since 1940 at the same time we have witnessed a rising tide of pornographic publication.

Over a period of just seven years, juvenile delinquency in the ten-to-seventeen age bracket rose by 115 per cent, compared with a population rise of 27 per cent.

Seven per cent of our total population under the age of

twenty-one was arrested for crime in 1959, as compared with *two* per cent of adults over twenty-one.

From all this grows a basic concern over the toll in human wreckage—the threat of this spreading sickness among the young people who will be our citizens of tomorrow.

It is understandable that there is no precise agreement as to the causes of juvenile crime. The problem is exceedingly complex. But one conclusion appears to be a matter of general agreement—that depraved actions result from poisoned minds. And there is evidence to show that nothing can be more vicious in poisoning the young mind than a diet of pornographic filth, whether it comes from a smut-laden newsstand, a shadowy peddler, or through the mails.

Psychiatrists have pointed out that a perfectly healthy child, exposed continually to the depravities of smutty material, can be turned into an immoral and distorted creature, if not an outright pervert.

Check with your police chief and you will probably find that, in his investigations of armed robbery, extortion, and forgery, he has often found that the guilty were early collectors of obscene matter.

Any experienced law-enforcement officer can provide the grim information that virtually every sex criminal has a record of an addiction to obscene literature and photographs.

The filth racketeers have learned that, among youngsters, they can develop addicts to obscene literature and pictures who will be not much different from the narcotics addict. Their objective is to get the child hooked, as is said of the dope addict, and keep him hooked. They feed him an array of trash carefully geared to successive stages of perversion.

Now, let me not be misunderstood. The proportion of our young people who actually permit themselves to become victimized by this racket is small. The great majority of our children will have nothing to do with it.

Normal teenagers have no interest in the obscene trash the racketeers would force on them. It disgusts them, just as it does their parents. Yet, the filth racketeers find encouragement. Through their mail-order solicitations they are able to seek out many young people who *are* unstable, who have not received the proper kind of parental guidance. And it is clear that the filth merchants, with huge profits to be gained, intend to continue trying to chip away hard at the fundamental good sense of young Americans.

The obscenity racketeers will yield only as they are literally driven out of business. Nothing will touch them short of constant action by the Post Office Department, constant pressure by the public for adequate legislation and prosecution, and the most rigorous punishment the courts can apply.

Our efforts to combat mail-order obscenity have received broad and highly gratifying support from the nation's newspapers, radio and television commentators, public-spirited organizations, and the members of Congress.

Hundreds of our leading newspapers have not only helped to advise the public of this menace in their news columns, but have carried editorials urging continued public support and co-operation.

Many television and radio commentators have spoken out, frequently and clearly, in support of this cause.

The Congress, in the past three years, has moved to meet this problem in a firm manner. An important amendment to the law, recommended by the Post Office Department and passed in 1958, has given us a valuable weapon. This revision makes it possible to prosecute not only at the point of mailing of obscene material, but in the communities where it is received—where the actual damage is done—and where citizens have the opportunity to express their standards of decency.

We have pressed its use to the fullest possible extent. The

144

first case following the legislation was at Boise, Idaho, and had to do with mailings made from California and Oregon. The offenders, a man and his wife, each received a ten-year prison sentence and a fine.

The 1958 statute asserts: "Every obscene, lewd, lascivious, or filthy book, pamphlet, picture, paper, letter, writing, print, or other publication of an indecent character . . . is declared to be nonmailable matter and shall not be conveyed in the mails or delivered from any post office or by any letter carrier. . . ."

In 1959, the House of Representatives voted a further strengthening of the mail-order obscenity statute. This legislation helps to close loopholes that have hampered our efforts to crack down on the mailers of obscene materials.

It passed overwhelmingly in the House—with, in fact, just one dissenting vote—and at this writing was ready for consideration by the Senate.

I would point out that the support of this subject is 100 per cent bipartisan. Members of both parties, and their leaders, not only have devoted much time to the legislative needs, but have done much to help alert their constituents to the insidious danger of this racket.

At the state level, too, there is a quickening of attention— a trend to more realistic legislation. Increasingly, the governors of the states are organizing state-wide efforts. The attorneys general of the states, in their annual convention, have endorsed a more positive program of action.

The mayors of many cities have organized co-ordinated drives by citizen committees. Many public-spirited groups have mobilized their members to help meet the challenge. Churches and religious organizations, which have long been in this battle, are giving their strength to its conduct.

Parents can help greatly if, when obscene material in the mail comes to their attention, they will send it to the local

145

postmaster, being sure to include the envelope. The evidence may also be mailed directly to Chief Postal Inspector, Washington 25, D.C., with a letter of complaint including the age, if a child was the addressee, and any other pertinent facts. Such complaints presented in sufficient volume by postal inspectors to U.S. Attorneys result in prosecutive action under the new venue provisions.

Strongly worded complaints are necessary proof that citizens of the community do not approve the use of the mail for the unsolicited offering of matter obscene or bordering on the obscene.

As a final and major catalyst of public participation, we invited the public to sit with us, by means of a committee of the highest standing, in the preliminary phases of making vital decisions.

Acceptance came not only from the religious organizations that always are in the forefront of the fight on vice; it came, as we had been confident that it would, also from the higher levels of the press and the publishing industry where quite properly the greatest forces are mustered to defend the freedoms granted to American citizens under the Constitution.

Nine distinguished and nationally known persons readily accepted membership on a group known as the Citizens' Advisory Committee on Literature, which was formally announced December 9, 1959. In many ways I consider the formation of this committee—and acceptance by its members—as a milestone of historic importance. Its initial members were: Douglas Black, President, Doubleday and Company, Inc., New York, N.Y.; Erwin D. Canham, President, Chamber of Commerce of the United States, Washington, D.C.; The Most Reverend William E. Cousins, Archbishop of Milwaukee, Milwaukee, Wisconsin; Roscoe Drummond, Columnist, New York *Herald Tribune*, Washington, D.C.; Miss Chloe Gifford, President, General Federation of Women's

Clubs, Washington, D.C.; Dr. Shane McCarthy, Executive Director, President's Council on Youth Fitness, Washington, D.C.; Dr. Julius Mark, Senior Rabbi, Temple Emanu-El, New York, N.Y.; Mrs. James Parker, President, National Congress of Parents & Teachers, Chicago, Illinois; Dr. Daniel Poling, Editor, the *Christian Herald,* New York, N.Y.

In announcing the committee, I made a brief statement that I think sums up our attitude toward the challenge of obscenity. It follows:

> I have today appointed a nine-member Citizens' Advisory Committee on Literature to help me reach decisions in matters relating to the mailability of materials where questions of obscenity arise.
>
> The Post Office Department is an agency of the people of the United States. It furnishes a public service utilized by the entire people of the country. The Post Office, therefore, has rightfully been charged by the Congress with the responsibility of meeting public standards in its operation.
>
> In accordance with these standards, specific legislation requires the Post Office Department to deny access to the mails of obscene materials that appeal to prurient interest with detrimental consequences to the public good.
>
> Any Postmaster General who would permit the Department to ignore completely this legal responsibility, as some critics propose, would be failing the duty of his office.
>
> At the same time, I am desirous of exercising this duty, as may be required, in a manner that fully reflects prevailing standards and judgment of the public *throughout* the country.
>
> To this end, it is my feeling that an Advisory Committee comprised of civic leaders representing a cross section of American life can be extremely helpful.
>
> The Citizens' Advisory Committee on Literature will in no sense of the word be a censorship body. Certainly, none of the distinguished citizens invited to serve as a member would accept if censorship were involved.
>
> The Postmaster General has no authority whatsoever to

147

prevent the publication of literature or its sale through channels other than the United States mails. The Committee, therefore, will be concerned solely with consulting with the Postmaster General, as the necessity may arise, as to whether or not a specific piece of literature submitted for mailing is obscene and should be denied access to the United States mails.

Any person with practical experience realizes, of course, that appointment of a committee has never completely solved a problem; likewise, that no single step ever won a campaign.

But sometimes evidences of understanding of grave problems, as presented by this committee, mark major steps in achieving of goals, and this is one of them.

It points clearly toward the day when an aroused public opinion can and will do for decency that which is impossible of accomplishment alone by passage of laws and even the most conscientious policing.

13

The Traffic in Dreams—
Mail Frauds

It was the boast of Joseph R. Weil, the notorious confidence man known as "The Yellow Kid," that he "never swindled an honest man." Obviously his claim was based on his belief that all victims were, like himself, trying to make quick profits by methods which, even though shady, met generally approved standards of honesty.

The fact is that confidence schemes comprise only a small portion of the huge field of fraudulent promotions which postal inspectors are constantly investigating. While some victims are susceptible to promises of "something for nothing," the vast majority are honest citizens who have implicit faith in the printed word and believe the promises of clever mail-order promoters in their adroitly worded advertisements.

Typical of these are needy persons, anxious to supplement their meager incomes, who fall victim to the knitting-machine and other work-at-home promotion. Also victimized are small businessmen, anxious to sell or obtain financing for their businesses, who are prey for promoters of the advance-fee scheme.

In the end the chiselers and purveyors of dreams usually are caught, but since justice can be administered only on the basis of carefully gathered evidence, they always get the first bites, and often tragically large ones, from seekers after the short cuts to wealth, health, and beauty.

The Postal Inspection Service has a category of about two hundred of the more common types of mail frauds, but they all have in common those desires. Therefore, the war on mail frauds is loaded against the inspectors in the first place by the very fact that so many persons want to believe the lies told to them.

It required long and hard work to track down an elusive pair of promoters of worthless stock in Oklahoma. When convicted, they received sentence of twelve years for their fakery, but in their span of operations—offering "shares" to the public—they sold such a volume that a final audit of their accounts revealed a shortage of $16 million—savings of individuals gone forever.

The fad for "quick and easy" weight reducing, without consulting doctors and featuring various types of pills and vibration machines that ostensibly require no diets or exercise, has led to a nationwide quackery that has cost disappointed users hundreds of millions a year.

In the field of business, a Chicago tire dealer was convicted in the past year and sentenced to two years in prison, plus five on probation, for a deal in which he offered "discounts" to independent service stations. He was convicted only after defrauding his customers by sending them junk tires to the tune of $700,000.

An advance-fee racket, operating out of Carroll, Iowa, presented to small businessmen a proposition whereby their businesses would be promptly sold by means of advertisements in newspapers throughout the United States. As evidence of good faith, the victims were required to post an advance fee, usually 5 per cent of the selling price, which would be returned if the business was not sold. The promoters obtained in excess of $250,000. No sales resulted and no fees were returned. Investigation by postal inspectors, working in cooperation with the United States Attorney, resulted in the conviction of nine persons in June, 1959, who received sentences ranging from eighteen months to two years' imprisonment.

As a footnote, Chief Postal Inspector Stephens has noted that there have been forty-nine indictments in the advance-fee promotion racket since it became popular.

Of course, when specific examples of these rackets are cited, the sums include only those which authorities can prove, based on complaints. The Inspection Service believes that swindles in the advance-fee racket have run as high as 50 million dollars in recent years.

Last year, postal inspectors arrested thirty persons in this field of criminal activity alone, obtained twenty indictments and won thirteen convictions. But how many were not caught?

The mails are too often used as a facility for selling worthless or up-priced matter—without official inspection or control of any kind. The promoter is protected from dissatisfied customers by distance and anonymity. Add to this the hypnotic effect of cunning advertising, and it is small wonder that fraudulent business by mail plagues us as a perennial problem.

In terms of the aged, the incidence of frailty and illness makes the medical-type fraud especially vicious. Where any type of medicine, treatment or device is offered through the mail, it should be considered suspect *per se*. Medicine and health products are available in the nearest drugstore, an establishment over which considerable official control is exercised.

Older people, on more mailing lists than younger ones, are subject to the full force of the vast circularization of direct-mail advertising. The mailing list is a working tool of the promoter who realizes that a certain percentage of people solicited will respond, no matter what is offered for sale.

Some worthy charities depend almost entirely on mail-order solicitations to support their work. However, there are also charity rackets operating by mail and the Post Office Department suggests that prospective donors make some inquiry before responding to pleas for contributions.

Charity rackets often use mailing lists of people their operators believe most likely to yield to solicitation. Many older persons of benevolent disposition answer the innumerable appeals that go through the mail. The promoters exploit flagrantly the finest impulses of the human heart. Any donor who gives locally can check on the use of his money. But when solicitation is by mail, there is a question of how much money ever reaches the beneficiary.

In a typical charity racket a promoter contracted with a nationally known benevolent organization to solicit funds ostensibly for care of the blind, with 87½ per cent of the amount raised to be retained by the promoter. Collecting around a million dollars a year, the promoter turns over to the blind association 12½ per cent. Obviously, no donor would ever "contribute" if he suspected almost ninety cents of his dollar went into the promoter's pocket.

The scheme is operated in typical fashion—the promoter pouring into the U.S. mails thousands of boxes of cheap, unordered greeting cards with a letter enclosure, apparently from the charitable organization, begging in the name of charity "please mail your contribution" in the enclosed envelope.

The receipt of such unordered merchandise with or without such an appeal should be considered suspect. Insofar as the promoter is concerned, he is successfully marketing, for far more than its actual value, shoddy material that no one would buy over the counter.

Very probably at some time you have received cheap, unordered merchandise in the mail with a request to pay for or return it. Greeting cards, books, neckties, pen and pencil sets, automobile key rings, "religious" medals and other cheap materials are being mailed today to people who did not order and do not want them. This stuff is so shoddy it is unsalable by other means. Many people wonder whether the law obliges them to return or pay for such matter.

If you do not want to pay for it, the material should be marked *Refused* on the cover and returned to the post office. The company will have to pay return postage which probably will assure that your name is removed from its mailing list so that you do not continue to receive similar material.

Postal regulations forbid the mailing of unordered merchandise by C.O.D. mail. However, some operators send such material anyhow, knowing that the addressee, having to pay the charges before delivery of a C.O.D. article, may unintentionally pay for it. If C.O.D.'s you have not ordered and do not want are addressed to you, notify your postmaster at once. Postal inspectors will investigate.

Since the law does not otherwise forbid the mailing of unordered merchandise, it has grown to such proportions the Post Office Department conducted a survey to determine the extent. Investigations by postal inspectors revealed many cases of fraud and near fraud. For instance, children and others who wrote to certain stamp companies for information found, when they began to receive stamp packages "on approval," that their names had been put on a mailing list. If they failed to return the stamps, the company sent severe dunning letters until payment was made. In some instances when the stamps were actually returned, some companies fraudulently claimed nonreceipt and continued to dun the addressee for payment.

Vending-machine rackets are prevalent. They are beamed at older people—retired, disabled, with small financial resources. It may be pointed out here that many mail-fraud schemes are not recognized by the victims as coming within the wide jurisdiction of the mail-fraud statute, because use of the mails is not apparent.

An operator and six salesmen recently received long prison sentences, but only after operating six years in many states because none of the victims realized that advertising and correspondence relating to the scheme were necessarily sent through the mails. When the matter finally came to the attention of postal inspectors, prompt investigations led to successful prosecution.

The first step in such a swindle is an attractive advertisement promising unreasonable profit for "part-time" effort. When the victim responds to the ad, the inevitable "salesman" calls, describing the wonderful money-making opportunities for a "reasonable" investment—whatever the victim can pay. He stresses the easy-payment plan, and offers exclusive territory, assistance in installing machines at locations already available, and a binding money-back guarantee if the customer is not completely satisfied.

Of course, this is fiction. The victim is likely never to see either the money or the "salesman" again. The "exclusive" territory promised is offered to dozens of victims. Few machines, if any, are actually furnished, and proprietors of "locations" are ignorant of the company, the salesman, and any contract permitting vending machines on the premises.

In some instances, the swindlers are in contact with purchasers for a time after the crime; in others they promptly vanish. Messages saying, "Where are my machines?" or "Please return my money, I am dissatisfied," are ignored or bring lulling replies, full of excuses of manufacturing and shipping delays.

These schemes are becoming more numerous every year. Postal inspectors investigate every swindle brought to their attention, and put the operators out of business by criminal prosecution.

Whatever the name—Pen Pal, Lonely Hearts, Matrimonial Clubs—all have the same intent: to engage in correspondence with members of the opposite sex, having in mind the possibility of marriage as one, if not the chief, motive. The number of lonely people whose lives are empty of romance provides a large market for the organizations offering mailing lists under the guise of lonely heart clubs.

A recent study indicated that over three hundred clubs were being operated, from those just beginning to the large established organizations with thousands of members. Prosecutions have not been extensive, but a number of clubs have ceased operations as a result of mail-fraud investigations.

Unscrupulous women resort to use of the mails to solicit funds from men, promising to join them if travel and other expenses are furnished. In a typical case, a woman in Los Angeles wrote to eight or more men simultaneously, arranging to receive her mail in private homes for a small fee and usually sending a boy for it so she could escape detection. When an investigation was started, she disappeared for weeks and then began an entirely new operation. She avoided apprehension for nearly two years.

A similar scheme, but somewhat more sinister, was operated by a man living in Texas with his wife and child. His sole income was derived from women he married after correspondence, the names procured through various clubs in California. He posed as a Texas rancher with interests in oil which could be developed with only another few thousand dollars. With this imminent fortune to be shared, he had no difficulty courting women and in a short time having them meet him in California. The victim was rushed into marriage by the tall, personable man. After a week or two of honeymooning he talked her out of all available assets. Then he provoked a scene of violence, sending her away so fearful of her life that no complaint was made. He acquired at least fifty thousand dollars a year from such activity, and few women could be found to admit to their ignominy. Postal inspectors put an end to this mail fraud and he was sentenced to three years in the penitentiary.

Many schemes do not go so far. Correspondence may lead to great protestations of love and to the planning of a first visit to get better acquainted. The victim learns that his (or her) lover has become ill or has perhaps suffered an accident en route. In either instance, the victim is urged to send money —and too often does.

Any question of loaning money or arranging a personal meeting should be contemplated with utmost caution. It must be realized that there are a sufficient number of dishonest persons who enroll in lonely heart clubs to make it questionable to correspond with strangers. Few, if any, clubs investigate applicants, and lists of names and addresses are available to anybody, including individuals whose motives are wholly fraudulent or sinister.

Of the endless variety of fraudulent schemes the most vicious is the sale of worthless medicines and therapeutic devices. The worst schemes advertise quick cures for cancer, tuberculosis, arthritis, diabetes, and other serious illness. Desperate victims try one "cure" after another, often delaying proper medical treatment until too late.

In the same category of criminal activity are the endless promotions that make quick fortunes from those "afflicted" with baldness, overweight, flat bust, or loss of virility. A leading racket is the promotion promising to cure obesity. Each scheme is good for several million dollars a year, paid for tonics and treatments known by medical experts, and the promoters, to be worthless.

The advice of medical authorities, however, is often not enough to cause the courts to bar the sale of such material. A typical example at the time of this writing is the continuing promotion on a wide scale of a device for reducing fat without effort—a rubber bowl containing an ordinary electric light bulb. Thousands complain to the Inspection Service that the device is absolutely worthless and the company refuses to refund the purchase price.

In the other direction are gimmicks for developing the bust—suction cups, dainty dumb bells, elastic exercisers, or hormone creams—wholly worthless and sometimes dangerous to use, in the opinion of doctors.

Medical frauds, taking advantage of human frailties, reap a golden harvest for quacks to such an extent that the Inspection Service maintains a unit of inspector specialists to investigate promotions of this type.

Music is one of the largest industries of the United States because it is one of our greatest hobbies. A fabulous amount of money is spent each year for musical instruments, sheet music, and phonograph records. Millions of people enjoy writing song lyrics or music as a hobby. This field has been invaded by the song shark who finds it easy to swindle many persons eager to have their lyrics or music published.

The song shark poses as a legitimate music publisher, or as a musician especially qualified to help arrange words and music so that music publishers will consider buying the finished song. Impressive advertisements offering to criticize lyrics or music appear in magazines. Whatever material is sent, even the simplest poem of a child, the song shark will praise, and assure the sender that for a moderate fee the company will be glad to collaborate. After the money is sent no service of any value is rendered. The amateur song writer has thrown his money away. Legitimate publishers never charge a fee in connection with publishing.

There are many industrious people who would like to earn extra money at home in their spare time. Beware of advertisements that promise good pay for easy, part-time work in your home. Be suspicious of schemes that demand money for information. Some are outright frauds. The advertiser may ask for a dollar or more and have no intention of sending anything in return. In one such case, two ex-convicts set up business by renting a post-office box and advertising in 350 newspapers nationwide that for one dollar information would be furnished showing how to make twenty-five dollars a week addressing envelopes. Postal inspectors learned of the scheme before the men could clean up and disappear. In a few weeks thirteen thousand letters, all containing dollar bills, were returned to senders. The men are serving long prison sentences.

In many other schemes you may receive something for your money, but it may be useless or of doubtful value. For a dollar one company furnishes a booklet promising to teach how to make more money; the booklet explains that honesty, judgment, leadership, etc. are necessary traits for success, and invites the reader to take a course in self-improvement. Another booklet for two dollars, promising to show how to attain wealth, carefully explains that hard work is the secret.

For a dollar, another company promised to send information on job opportunities in a certain part of the country. The persons who sent their dollar received only a part of a newspaper classified-ad section.

Many of the home mail-addressing jobs are actually chain-letter schemes. If you answer the ad, you may receive a letter stating that a dollar will bring you information and material for making money addressing mail. If you send a dollar, you receive identical copies of the same letter you answered. The only way to get your money back is to send these letters out to other victims.

Although lottery in the United States is prohibited by Federal law, fortunes are made every year from lottery enterprises. The huge sums of money are never made by those who buy lottery tickets but by the big-name crooks who counterfeit tickets of lotteries being run in foreign countries, or who distribute tickets on fake lotteries. For instance, genuine tickets of the Irish Hospital Sweepstakes are smuggled into the United States, but since they can be counterfeited easily, it is questionable whether the purchaser of a ticket pays for one that is genuine. Those persons who distribute genuine tickets are also breaking the law. Money paid for these tickets frequently is not forwarded to the Sweepstakes officials. A world-wide investigation by the Postal Inspection Service proved also that some Sweepstakes officials pocket some of the money.

As apparent as these facts may seem, thousands of Americans pay millions of dollars into the pockets of criminals every year.

In the roaring 20's and 30's some of the most notorious gangsters organized gigantic lottery rings. As much as 200 million dollars a year was swindled from gullible citizens who thought they were buying chances to win big cash prizes. No big cash prizes were ever paid, just a few small come-on payments. Postal inspectors have stamped out the big lottery rings, but so long as sweepstake and other lottery tickets are sold, fake and counterfeit tickets will also be available.

The Post Office Department warns against participation in chain-letter schemes. Any chain letter that requires any payment of value is illegal under the Federal lottery statute.

A lottery is defined as a scheme whereby something of value is paid for the chance of winning a prize. Many persons do not realize that in addition to violating the lottery law, chain letters are also fraudulent in that they seem to promise the possibility of large returns for a small investment. In some instances a few persons entering the scheme at the beginning receive more than they put in, but never the large sums promised. The great majority of participants receive nothing at all, but lose their entire investment. Such an outcome is inevitable as the supply of interested persons is soon exhausted, and the greater the amount to be invested, the sooner the saturation point will be reached.

When chain letters are discovered in the mails, postal inspectors look into the likelihood of outright fraud. Individuals or organized groups often start a chain circulating by printing thousands of letters with their own names on top. An individual recently began one chain by mailing ten thousand letters with his own name first.

As with other mailed materials that smack of fraud, the person who receives these letters will be wise—and helpful —to turn them over to his postmaster for investigation.

PART III

14

The Challenge of Change

The subsequent chapters of this book contain some accounts of developments in modernizing the postal service that have the same dream-world quality as stories of developments in missile and satellite work, but preceding and underlying the outward dramas there has been a change of concept and in operations that has revolutionized the postal service.

To the public which uses, supports and as yet subsidizes its postal service out of tax payments, this is personal, intimate, and vital. It is a great adventure in progress that touches every American now and in his future.

We live by communications and at any moment we may

165

find that we survive because of them. When the Post Office Department improves the speed and reliability of communications, it makes a direct contribution to the defense preparations of other Departments of Government and, unlike them, it brings a new standard of service to the day-to-day life of every American.

Fantastic developments in facsimile mail, speed-ups in intercity transit, "automatic post offices"—all of these are of vital importance. Yet they rest upon organization, administration, and the development of new concepts.

In the postal service, our proudest achievement, I feel, is the improvement in organization and research. Stunts cannot take the place of service. There is no detail that is unimportant in working toward our goal of overnight delivery service for all letter mail moving in or between our major population centers.

This is our job. Equally important is the determination that—under our political system in which changes invariably must occur in the executive machinery of government departments—we leave behind for the next team chosen to run the postal service a strong and fully modern foundation on which sound future progress can be built.

Economists have written millions of words about the "management society" developed in the American economy as part of its fantastic growth—the system of continuity in vital businesses that is freed from any risk of radical changes through death or alterations at the top.

It seems to me that the running of the enormous business that is the United States Postal Service imposes a duty not only to meet the best standards of a management society but to give leadership to it in all the fields of operations, research, development, and public relations.

It has been often reported that a railroad tycoon of the last century once exclaimed, "The public be damned!" Much was made of this phrase and its connotations as applied to business in the frenetic debates that characterized the early years of the New Deal.

Yet as a businessman, a member of the public who has worked his own way from the bottom of the ladder to some positions of responsibility in private life, I can state truthfully and with total objectivity this conclusion, which was presented in essence in Chapter One:

In all my prior experience and dealings with finance, business, sales, and labor relations, I had never seen anything to compare with the general attitude of our own postal service toward its public responsibilities on the day that, as a fresh "political appointee," I undertook the job as Postmaster General. Not only was the public "damned" by inefficiency, patronage, and poor concepts; it was "damned" by procedures that differed in 1952 very little from those of 1900.

In the largest post offices, mail still was sorted by men standing before racks of boxes, doing this chore exactly as it had been done before the Civil War. Most of the major post-office buildings were monuments in stone to political patronage, designed more for solid appearance on the outside than for efficient work within. The Congress had not appropriated any funds to build new post offices since 1938.

Visits to various post offices revealed absence rates running as high as one third of total employment. A generally underpaid and underprivileged employee group was fighting mad over inequities in promotion and opportunity, and consequently used its own organized strength to "lobby" in Congress for the honest deal its own management should have provided. And in a minority but surprisingly large number of cases, aggressive members of the Congress could and did use the Post Office as a political weapon back home.

Why try to change it? the question was asked. More importantly, few if any persons outside President Eisenhower's own small "family" really expected a sincere effort at change.

From a political standpoint, I was a "traditional" appointee to the job. I had been active in politics as an avocation for all of my adult life, not as an office seeker, but as a Republican worker first in my home community of Flint, Michigan, then in the state, and finally as Chairman of the Republican National Committee, when I was privileged to direct the campaign of General Eisenhower and Candidates for the U.S. Congress. The stage apparently was set, in the view of the long-entrenched party whose candidate for the President was defeated by President Eisenhower, for the Republican Party to re-entrench itself by traditional placement of strategic state, city, and ward leaders in the control and the principal jobs of the postal service.

They could not understand that we meant what we said. Now, after more than seven years of activity, I think our works speak for us, and prove what we meant when we said three things:

1. The President had no such views, and would not have tolerated this attitude had it been advanced by any of his supporters.
2. I held no such views.
3. Finally, there existed, in the dark recesses of pigeon-holed reports, a valuable study of the postal service prepared by one of the hard-hitting task forces of the Hoover Commission for the Reorganization of Government.

Many "Hoover Reports" on government had been filed. We determined that this one should be made a living thing as the basis for a new concept and new activities. On it we built.

After I had been invited to serve as Postmaster General, I went to Washington and took rooms in a hotel there. I read mountains of reports and memoranda, freely supplied by Jesse

168

M. Donaldson, my immediate predecessor. Mr. Donaldson, a career man in the postal service, was the exception to the political appointment system in recent years, a circumstance that made him perhaps more vulnerable to political pressures than otherwise, since he owed the culminating years of his career to the political leaders who gave him his office, and who in turn felt no indebtedness to him.

As a second step in preliminary studies, I requested the Hoover Commission to "lend" to me two of the key business survey experts who had directed the study of the postal service, which they did, despite the sacrifices in time required of these men. Finally, after these outside experts prepared a list of names of skilled, loyal and forward-looking men within the Post Office Department itself, I "borrowed" two of these.

As a team of five, we started the blueprint of a revised and modern postal system, and a program of legislation to present to the Congress as a first step in putting it into effect. As a footnote, the legislative program, backed by the President, later was enacted, as well as many subsequent amendments designed to keep pace with the work we were accomplishing—all within the limits of practical change at the time.

However, ideas and plans are no better than the persons who must implement them with their own concepts and carry them through. We drew up lists of the types of men needed to fill the key jobs. Such action was without precedent. For the first time in Post Office history, the new Postmaster General of a party long out of office filled the key positions in the Post Office Department with qualified men chosen for their experience and skill in handling similar jobs in industry.

The next step was to translate organization into positive —yes, revolutionary—action.

Under structural reorganization made by Mr. Donaldson,

the Department had five key positions to be filled by appointment from outside, in addition to my own—the Deputy Postmaster General, and four Assistant Postmaster Generals heading the departments of Operations, Transportation, Facilities, and Finance.

It was my purpose to find men for these responsibilities who could apply the genius of business thinking and leadership to the tremendous job we faced. My success in gaining the help of such men was one of the most gratifying and inspiring experiences of my life.

My first appointment was that of Charles R. Hook, Jr., as Deputy Postmaster General.

Mr. Hook, a vice president of the Chesapeake & Ohio Railroad, was a recognized authority on management and personnel. He was given the all-important assignment of recommending top representatives of business and industry to head the important positions on the Postmaster General's staff.

Norman R. Abrams, a director and vice president of Congoleum-Nairn, Inc., agreed to become the Assistant Postmaster General heading up our Bureau of Operations, which is in charge of the more than thirty-six thousand post offices in the country.

John C. Allen, general traffic manager of Sears, Roebuck & Company, accepted the position of Assistant Postmaster General for our Bureau of Transportation which has to do with the moving of the mails between the post offices of the country.

I invited Gerald F. Healey, a long-time personal friend and an outstanding realty expert from Flint, Michigan, to study our Bureau of Facilities which is concerned with the vast real-estate operations of the Post Office Department.

Mr. Healy spent three months in doing so and then recommended the appointment of Ormonde A. Kieb, an experienced realtor from New Jersey, and former president of the

Institute of Real Estate Management, which is part of the National Association of Real Estate Boards, as the Assistant Postmaster General in charge of our Bureau of Facilities.

Albert J. Robertson, a prominent banker from Des Moines, Iowa, who was senior vice president and director of the Iowa–Des Moines National Bank and a director of other Iowa banks, was recommended to us by the American Bankers Association, and accepted the appointment of Assistant Postmaster General in charge of our Bureau of Finance.

Ross Rizley, a former Congressman from Oklahoma and an outstanding lawyer, became the Department's Solicitor, a title later changed to General Counsel.

A distinguished career postal employee, as previously noted, David H. Stephens, was appointed Chief Inspector.

Ben H. Guill, a former Congressman from Texas, became my Executive Assistant in charge of Congressional relationships.

L. Rohe Walter of New York, an advertising and public relations expert, was chosen as my Special Assistant for Public Relations, a newly established office. Mr. Walter's sole instructions were to use the training of his profession to give the public maximum understanding of the responsibility of the Post Office Department and, by sifting all reactions—however trivial some might seem—to provide guides for us in improving service and for the public in its most efficient use.

With this staff of outstanding business and professional men we were early equipped to tackle the vast reorganization and operating problems.

Additionally, we were aided by a group of distinguished American business and professional leaders who accepted appointment by the President on the Post Office Department Advisory Board. These included: Honorable Consuelo Northrop Bailey, attorney and Speaker of the House of Representatives, Vermont State Legislature; Richard E. Berlin,

171

President, the Hearst Corporation; John S. Coleman, President, Burroughs Corporation; Richard J. Gray, President, Building and Construction Trades Department, American Federation of Labor; Curtis W. McGraw, chairman of the board and president, McGraw-Hill Publishing Co.; Rowland Jones, Jr., President, American Retail Federation; and Charles M. White, President, Republic Steel Corporation.

Messrs. Jones, White, Berlin and Gray have served continuously as members of this Board. Jack Rohe Howard, president of Scripps-Howard Newspapers; James H. S. Ellis, retired advertising executive of Reno, Nevada, and Ormond E. Hunt, director of General Motors Corporation, have succeeded Messrs. Coleman and McGraw, who have died, and Mrs. Bailey, who resigned to become Secretary of State of Vermont.

The management firm of Robert Heller & Associates, Inc., had been engaged by the task force of the Hoover Commission to study the needs of the Post Office Department. We continued to employ this competent group to assist us in the reorganization of the Department.

Some of the men on the original top staff have served with me during the entire past seven and a half years. Others on the original staff and several who joined us later have been invited to occupy other important positions in the Government. These include Mr. Robertson who is Chairman of the Federal Home Loan Bank Board; Mr. Rizley is a Federal Judge; Maurice H. Stans is the Director of the Budget; Eugene J. Lyons is Special Assistant to the President for Personnel Management; Edson O. Sessions is Ambassador to Finland; Abe McGregor Goff is a member of the Interstate Commerce Commission; and Ben H. Guill served for several years as Vice Chairman of the Maritime Commission. Jeffrey P. Hillelson is Acting Postmaster of Kansas City, Missouri, and

Harry L. Brookshire is Minority Clerk for the House of Representatives.

In certain instances the members of my original top staff were succeeded by equally capable men likewise chosen from business and industry.

Mr. Stans succeeded Mr. Hook as Deputy Postmaster General on October 1, 1955, and during the following two years reorganized the accounting procedures of the Department.

Mr. Sessions, a nationally known management engineer, suceeded Mr. Stans and during his two years in office gave brilliant direction to the Department's modernization program.

John M. McKibbin, a former vice president of Westinghouse, the present Deputy Postmaster General, joined the Department in February of 1957 as head of our Bureau of Operations and became the Deputy in November of 1959. He has been primarily responsible for the development of the vitally important "Metro Plan" whereby letters mailed by 5:00 P.M. within ninety metropolitan areas having a population of 150 million are delivered the next day anywhere within the area.

Bert B. Barnes, the present Assistant Postmaster General heading the Bureau of Operations, is a long-time career postal employee whose practical experience and devotion have been of inestimable value to us since 1953.

E. George Siedle, who was general traffic manager of Armstrong Cork Company succeeded Mr. Allen as Assistant Postmaster General of the Bureau of Transportation.

George M. Moore who has followed Mr. Siedle in this post, also is doing an outstanding job in handling the Department's relationships with the common carriers which transport the mails between post offices. Mr. Moore served in several important Government positions before joining us, notably on

173

the Staff of the House Post Office, and as a Member of the Civil Service Commission.

Hyde Gillette, a former partner in the Chicago investment banking firm of Glore, Forgan & Company, is the Assistant Postmaster General heading the Bureau of Finance. He has established accounting and record-keeping procedures and a modern controllership over the Department's complicated fiscal matters which is unequaled in Government.

Rollin D. Barnard, the present Assistant Postmaster General for Facilities, came to the Department from his business as a realtor in Denver and, until his appointment in March of 1959, served as Mr. Kieb's deputy. Much of the Department's success in advancing its modernization and construction programs is due to his untiring work and leadership.

Frank Barr, a former utility executive from Wichita, Kansas, first served the Department as its Regional Operations Director for the Wichita Region. His outstanding accomplishments in field management, plus his background of personnel work for industry and the Army, made him the logical successor to Eugene Lyons as Assistant Postmaster General, Bureau of Personnel.

Herbert B. Warburton has been our General Counsel since February, 1958. A former Congressman from Delaware, he is uniquely equipped to work with the Congress on legislative matters affecting the Department. His assistance in our drive against mail-order obscenity is also a great public service.

Wade S. Plummer, Director of the Office of Research and Engineering since March of 1959, is an experienced industrial engineer and administrator. His objectivity and drive have made notable contributions to the Department's modernization efforts.

Nyle M. Jackson, my Executive Assistant since May of 1959, handles the all-important day-by-day relationships with the Congress. His previous experience on the "Hill" in various administrative capacities ideally equip him for this important liaison work.

Mrs. Hattie M. Traver, who previously was my secretary in Flint, has been my Administrative Assistant throughout these seven and one-half years. Her outstanding competence and deep sense of personal responsibility have been invaluable to me in the administration of my office; and her direction of my immediate office staff has assured a high morale and efficient operation.

Mrs. Cecil M. Harden, a former Member of Congress from Indiana, and Member, House Post Office and Civil Service Committee, became my Special Assistant for Women in March of 1959. Since then she has given able direction to the recruitment of women; to matters affecting the Department's fifty thousand women postal employees; and to speaking engagements before women's groups in behalf of the Department's drive against mail-order obscenity.

Thus the all-important question of key management was happily solved. There remained for the "team" thereby created the equally vital task of translating purposes and plans into action that would bring results.

The challenge that faced the entire service in 1953 was one of making the Post Office as efficient as the economy it serves in the mid-twentieth-century, while not only holding on to but improving the traditions of freedom of communications and the immense human values of loyalty in the service.

We must provide ever faster service, develop more efficient internal organization, and reach for maximum economy by the use of modern tools and the development of a new sense of responsibility.

Transportation developments help us to serve the public by ever faster intercity communications, and mechanization helps greatly the task of local delivery. We have made great progress in both. But the heart of the postal service is the inner handling of the mail—its collection, sorting and distribution. And no amount of nostalgia over the good old days can diminish that responsibility, any more than American business, holding to the old ways, can fall behind the public's demands without paying the price of failure.

This challenge called for revolutionary changes *inside the post offices* themselves, for vast alterations in transportation, and most of all for new concepts upon which to build.

It likewise called for new organization in a nationwide tying together of the individual post offices. Detailed descriptions of this new type of business improvement are too complicated for treatment here, and of interest only in terms of service. But here are some summaries of their meaning to the individual Amercian when he consigns to the postal service his cumulative 175 million letters or parcels each day.

You as a patron of the postal service are one of 180 million individuals who are our customers and our employers. Unless you are one person in six living in a fairly remote locale outside of a "metropolitan area," you are receiving all mail sent to you within your area on the day after it is posted.

On August 21, 1958, we set this next-day delivery as a goal for metropolitan areas and now we are working toward next-day delivery everywhere, from one side of the country to the other. The progress we have made has been achieved by decentralization of authority and displacement of outmoded operations, plus a gigantic task of incorporating new techniques and machines to help out human hands.

Likewise, and perhaps more importantly, we have broken the old chains that tied the postal service to an idea of bureaucracy that was a sacred cow and none of the public's business except to pay the bills. I think that few users of postal facilities realize what contributions have been made to this new concept by otherwise busy men—individuals only too glad to help improve this vital service in the old American tradition of service without compensation or special advantage to themselves or their businesses.

We have a group, appointed by President Eisenhower, known as the Post Office Department Advisory Board—men from organizations national in size and scope, and with deep experience in the problems we needed to solve—who from time to time review our work, criticize it and make suggestions. They are an active, interested group, not a figurehead.

Their names were listed in a previous chapter and show, I believe, that we work with the advice of groups and businesses who have much to contribute and who in the past have sometimes represented the severest critics of the postal service.

This board has observed closely all phases of the Department's research and development program and, during regularly scheduled meetings with key postal officials, reviewed its progress. We in the Department have benefited from the counsel and many valued contributions of the Advisory Board over the years in which it has worked with us.

Such support has helped us to create new methods— heartily welcomed by the Congress—that cut the red tape of bureaucratic control exercised by Washington over the entire postal service. We have been determined to make impossible the recurrence of patronage situations of other years such as the practice in some cities of going toward leaders for recruitment of the necessary extra "substitutes" in rush periods such as Christmas. Unbelievable as it sounds, there were times in New York and other cities when illiterates were sent to the post offices to pick up the "gravy jobs," and in turn to contribute a part of their earnings to the political bosses.

177

Now the Post Office Department runs its own business, as a business, within the limits permitted by Congress, and we pray that it may continue to do so.

The Metropolitan Area Service Improvement Project—in Post Office terminology—now is a definite operating entity, supervised and staffed by men with all the authority and ability required to do the job the public deserves. No longer must every procedural question stream back to Washington.

Postmasters such as Robert K. Christenberry in New York City and Otto K. Olesen in Los Angeles are typical of postal administrators who have developed their management abilities in the tough school of business leadership. Postmaster Christenberry directs an operation which has thirty-five thousand employees and an annual revenue of 253 million dollars; Postmaster Olesen has twenty thousand employees and an annual volume of 177 million dollars. Only a small percentage of business firms are of such a size. It is essential that the Post Office be able to attract men such as these to its service.

A metropolitan area may be pictured by comparison with department-store or other delivery zones around American cities. It may be twenty miles in diameter or it may extend for fifty, depending on concentration of population. It means constant abolition of little independent post offices and their reorganization as branches or substations of each central office.

Thus Greenwich, Connecticut, the Oranges in New Jersey, and Yonkers, New York, are part of the area or local service of Greater New York, with the same intra-area fast service. The same is true of the areas around Chicago, San Francisco, St. Louis, New Orleans or the other metropolitan centers of the United States.

Since some of the areas are quite close to each other, a few supervisory functions were combined in Postal Service Centers located in the fifty-five largest post offices to cut down overhead for area work. This does not make one area secondary to another, but co-ordinates and improves the services of all.

Finally, we divide the former Washington control into fifteen segments officially called Regions. These are the nerve centers and controls for all operations, transportation and continuous testing for the improvement of services. They are headed by Regional Operations Directors, served by Field Service Officers and Mobile Service Officers who can act on the spot to correct errors in service or make improvements without delay.

Supported by this modern organization, service to the individual member of the public is centered most directly on the organization and improvement within his local post office. We turn next to a brief illustration of what has been done in this field.

Standing in the center of a fourteen-acre site five minutes from the heart of Providence, Rhode Island, close by the famous old Post Road, is a modernistic building with eight flaring roof sections. Scheduled to open in 1960, it is destined to be known in our history as the world's first "automatic post office." Its name is "Turnkey," and it embodies every practical modern mechanized feature. And in the planning stage at this writing is the second, named "Gateway," at Oakland, California.

These revolutionary post offices are built to accommodate every mechanical and electronic device practicable as replacement for human legs and hands at the post offices of the foreseeable future, regardless of the changes in distribution of mail by new techniques involving the use of air, rail, or highway transport.

Both are patterned in large part on modernization work done insofar as possible in the post office at Washington, D.C., which was dedicated in its new form (completely modernized insofar as possible in an existing building) on March 3, 1959. As an example of the radical changes involved in the first work at Washington, some equipment in use for more than a century was junked and replaced by new mechanical or electronic equipment.

However, Turnkey will remain unique because, while it is a working post office, it is designed also as the experimental base for the anticipated flow of vastly improved machines and operations still to come in the future with full development of the modernization program. What we have done in the past seven years of this Administration is considered foundational, not final.

The location at Providence was selected because of the great need for modernized postal facilities there, and further because it is fairly typical of many American communities. This post office serves primarily the principal city in Rhode Island, and is the distributing center for about one hundred other cities and towns.

In its effect on the area, it is symbolic of many other post office buildings newly completed, or planned, under this program.

These outstandingly designed new structures often bring about a notable change in the spirit and appearance of the whole community in which they are located. In revitalizing and beautifying their locale, they often stimulate its development far beyond the immediate effects of the improved postal service. They make a pronounced social and economic contribution to the community and at no increased expense to the taxpayer.

The new Providence Post Office is divided roughly into two main areas—first and smaller, the public lobby and, second, a work area about the size of two football fields.

In the lobby the local users will see an array of self-help

machines including many completed in the last year or two. Here are the familiar stamp-vending machines, but in new guises that almost make of them miniature sales departments.

Some of these machines automatically weigh and stamp letters and parcels, make change automatically, and supply most of the other common postal services, including regular and airmail stamps, books of stamps and postal cards. In fact, the "automatic" customer service has been developed to a point where the Department has manufactured prototypes of always-open branch post offices, unattended, complete with parcel-post-acceptance machines and lockboxes. These are designed as substations for installation in our rapidly growing suburban areas.

However, the dramatic changes embodied in Turnkey are in the vast work area seldom seen by the public, and attended by relatively few employees.

The first breath-taking impression of this work area is given by a twenty-six-foot control tower, surmounted by a glass room for key supervisors. From this tower, essential orders flow to men and to machines while literally miles of conveyors tie together the complex operations that have threatened to founder older post offices and their staffs.

There are five major operations combined in this unprecedented development, named (1) Mailflo, (2) Culling, (3) Facing and Canceling, (4) Automatic Sorting, and (5) Parcel Sorting. Each operation was, as recently as a decade ago, done with only slight variations from the manner evolved in the past century, primarily by men and women handling monotonously repetitious chores as the postal load of the country rose up to swamp them. Many postal workers still have to operate in cluttered elbow-to-elbow spaces, where the handlers fight their way through snarled passageways, often under antiquated lights, with poor ventilation and hardly ever any air conditioning.

By contrast Turnkey is a quiet model of efficiency where workers direct machines that do the more arduous work faster and at less cost.

Here are thumbnail descriptions of the five major operations that make up this model post office:

MAILFLO:

Mailflo looks at first glance much like any other constantly moving conveyor twisting its way through a predesignated course. Yet it is probably the most important of all the new developments, when the many modern thinking mechanisms are added to it. The trick in this adaptation of Mailflo is the use of letter trays that resemble a small boy's dream of a toy train system, as they enter and leave the conyevor in response to electrical signals.

Unsorted letter mail starts at the beginning of Mailflo in trays "ordered" by a supervisor to proceed to designated work or storage areas. The trays carry their own switching orders in coded devices attached to them—"precoded elements," these are called. At the proper point along the main line, each tray turns onto a branch line to take its load to the place ordered in advance.

People take over from machines in the sorting area, but Mailflo then picks up the trays of letters designated for transfer to trains or airplanes or trucks. In a matter of minutes this sorted mail is sacked and ready to go.

Meanwhile, in the control tower, one man with a microphone attached to a loudspeaker gives the basic directions for Mailflo, much as the control tower of a great airport directs plane movements, having learned by heart the intricate schedules of planes and trains leaving for various parts of the country, and being advised hourly of any changes in them. Thus the sorted mail moves on a minute-to-minute schedule, saving hours over the former haphazard system.

CULLING:

First stop on Mailflo is the Culling Department where all mail deposited in Providence and its one hundred satellite stations must be handled. This act of "culling," one of the most tedious of jobs, ordinarily has been done by the repetitious labor of ranks of men picking up and handling each individual piece of mail—costly, inefficient, humdrum, and unchanged.

At Turnkey, and rapidly going into older post offices, the new Culling System seems almost to think for itself, from the moment that upturned mail sacks dump their loads of unsorted mail—letters, packages, even hotel keys—into a machine resembling a large tank. This basic unit at Turnkey is 17 feet long and 6 feet high. It does the work under the quiet, skilled supervision of two operators.

From the first receiving machine the mail is sent over a series of vibrating tables that shake it out until no piece lies on top of another. Thus prepared, the mail goes over a tent-shaped slide, where moving arms nudge packages and thick pieces of mail off the table into a bulk hopper, while letters and postal cards fall through slots to a lower conveyor belt. The heavy pieces go their own way for individual handling, but the regular mail automatically is sorted again and again until relatively similar sizes stand neatly in trays, where they get another vibration treatment to bring them into alignment for the next automatic operation of Facing and Canceling.

FACING AND CANCELING:

Here our new postal ideas plunge headlong into the amazing world of electronics, jumping in one leap from colonial days to the world of tomorrow. As recently as yesterday there had been only one major advance over age-old procedures—the automatic canceling machine—and prior to the feeding of letters and cards into these machines, the human hand was the only known tool.

First in the process of automatic culling is a rapidly moving assemblage of amazing electric eyes and belts spinning on rollers. It receives the letters and cards, instantaneously scans each one, and sends each into grooves with the stamp on each in proper position for canceling—even making allowances for wide variation in the location of stamps. While doing this job it automatically rejects and sends into another compartment unstamped mail, pre-canceled mail or wrongly stamped envelopes. There is a channel for every type of mail and seven letters or postcards are canceled every second.

AUTOMATIC SORTING:

Most of us have nostalgic memories of waiting in a post office in some small community for our mail, watching while the postmaster deftly flipped letters into individual boxes. But nostalgia turns into a nightmare in the great central post offices of the twentieth century when hundreds of clerks must sit in rows doing the job in the same manner as the Colonial postmaster in Boston whose original sorting desk is in our museum.

Sorting of mail for despatch under the old system has two absolutely unavoidable limitations, the speed of the man's eyes and hands, and the reach of his arms.

By contrast, at Turnkey, picture six girls sitting at desks in a large, well-lighted room, each with an electric keyboard in front of her, with an automatic conveyor silently delivering its trays of canceled letters one by one on an automatic track across each desk at the rate of fifty a minute, or a total of eighteen thousand an hour to this one group of girls.

The keyboards operated by each girl have code signals for three hundred different destinations for the letters. Each board controls all three hundred; there is no running back and forth. There is no reaching, no strain.

At the order given by an operator who presses the right

keys, each individual letter is taken on by the conveyor to be dropped into the assigned area box, from which the mail in bulk can be taken at intervals to be "sacked" and sent on to its destination.

All of this procedure sounds so simple that it belies the complex development that made it possible, centering around an electronic "memory brain" that must guide and control every single piece of mail in accordance with instructions relayed through the keyboards.

PARCEL SORTING:

It was stated earlier that more than *one billion* pieces of parcel post go through our postal system each year. Each is as important as a letter in that it must be delivered in good condition to an individual addressee.

Even in smaller post offices the handling of the parcel business reaches huge proportions, and in the archaic forms it is backbreaking, as well as time-consuming. One of the more common older forms of sorting parcel post was to dump a consignment of parcels into an inclined trough, down which they would slowly slide as men rummaged through them, picked up each individual piece, read the address and then dropped the parcel into an open bag for delivery to its next sorting station. Both with letters and parcel post, this retransiting and resorting would occur anywhere from three to twenty times or more.

Now we can state that, not only at Turnkey, where the system has been brought to the highest point of efficiency yet achieved, but also in most major post offices, a system known as "The Webb Machine" has taken much of the individual labor out of the job, speeded it immeasurably and cut costs.

Parcels, as well as letters arrive at post offices in large bags designed in size and weight capacity for handling by strong men in some still necessary operations. The contents of these bags are removed by men, but here the manual operation ends, as they are dumped on a belt conveyor of the electronically controlled sorting machine.

The parcels are taken by the belt to a chute and dropped into "positioning areas," where they are placed, face up for easy reading, on individual little pallets that travel over short conveyor systems to "coding stations." As each individual parcel passes under the eye of a sorting clerk, he simply reads the address and presses a code button sending the parcel, still on its pallet, along to the proper station. When each pallet arrives at the ordered destination, the electronic brain tilts it and slides the parcel into the ordered hopper, from which it is delivered to the next sacking area either for sending to another post office or for local delivery.

One parcel-post machine has six conveyors and six coding stations through which it handles 14,400 parcels an hour.

I know very well that descriptions of great new developments of efficiency in automation and mechanization immediately raise the question of their possible results on jobs for people. Questions are asked as to the number of persons displaced by machines or released from jobs in which they have worked a lifetime.

Must efficiency and speed be achieved at the cost of present jobs?

The answer is no.

With all of the striving toward making the postal service better, faster and more economical in the past eight years, no one has been laid off simply because his job was "taken over by a machine." No one has been transferred merely to keep him on the payroll for humanitarian reasons. Many jobs—as a result of these improvements—are better than the older ones, providing higher pay for more skilled work.

It will, however, greatly reduce the number of new employees needed to process the ever-increasing volume of mail in the future.

The postal service, like the country itself, is growing so fast that the maximum development of new operating efficiencies is the minimum required as far into the future as we can foresee.

In seeking this sound objective, the postal service will stand as a growing reservoir of better job opportunities.

15

A Postal Service to Meet Today's Demands

On June 8, 1959, the guided missile submarine U.S.S. *Barbero*, surfaced in the Caribbean Sea and fired a Regulus missile, aimed at the United States. Within a few minutes the guided missile landed at the Naval Air Auxiliary Station at Mayport, Florida, its landing wheels down under remote control, with a braking parachute flaring out from its tail.

The Regulus could have carried an atomic bomb, but it did not. There was no explosion, and relatively little fanfare. Instead, an airfield jeep neatly fastened a towline to the missile's nose and pulled the huge, sleek, unmanned aircraft to a parking area, where it was opened.

Out of the Regulus was taken a consignment of three thousand letters, completing a successful experiment in delivery of mail by guided missile. Within a few hours, Letter No. 1 in the Regulus was delivered personally to President Eisenhower in the White House by letter carrier Noble Upperman of the Washington, D.C., Post Office.

The Post Office Department, in this experiment, had used a major development of the U.S. Navy in guided missiles for the peaceful purpose of delivering mail, demonstrating again its interest in adopting to its own needs the advances made by other agencies of the Government.

Already, however, the question exists as to whether this example in itself is not outmoded, as will be described further in a chapter on microwave facsimile transmission of written messages.

Whatever the answers developed in the future, the thoughts of those of us who witnessed the Regulus demonstration darted back through a kaleidoscope of the past:

There was the first train delivery of mail between Camden and Amboy, New Jersey, in 1832.

Nineteen years earlier, the steamship *Savannah,* first steamer to cross the Atlantic Ocean, had sailed out of Savannah, Georgia, for Liverpool, England, on its historic twenty-seven-day voyage, and aboard *Savannah* was a consignment of mail in the care of Nathaniel Crane, on leave from his normal work of supervising the stagecoach mail service between Washington and Philadelphia.

There had been the Pony Express; there had been the airmail service, with its beginnings at Mineola, Long Island.

And there had been a single element that tied all of these together: It was the fact that mail contracts had been so interlocked with American transportation as to be inseparable in development.

More than a century ago it was commonplace for stage lines in newly developing territory to seek out mail contracts as a first guarantee of operating expenses. The stages operated by Wells Fargo and the Overland Stage Coach Company, connecting the Far West with the East, bore in gilt lettering on their doors: "U.S. Mail."

Railroad trains have carried this symbol on their mail cars from the time of the Civil War onward. The legend U.S. Mail was burned into the saddlebags of Pony Express couriers and engraved on the stocks of the rifles and pistols carried to protect the mail. It was forged into the iron boxes designed to fit underneath stagecoach seats. It was painted on the Curtiss Jennies, the Bleriots, the DeHavilands and other early open-cockpit airplanes that inaugurated the Air Mail Service.

In the 1890's—with belated recognition of the need of the United States for a merchant marine under the American flag —it was mail contracts that provided the original subsidy backing the historic Pacific Mail Steamship Company, the Brazil Steamship Company and the "Red D" lines.

In the long history of transportation development in our country, we always find one inescapable conclusion, coupled with a question that leads to interminable debate, even today.

The conclusion is that mail contracts have done more than any other factor to give assured income on which much of the great network of American public-service transportation has been erected.

The question is how to draw the line between actual costs of transportation paid by the public through postal contracts with carriers and the additional support desired by these common carriers from the Government, which is called "subsidy."

This volume is no place in which to set forth a complicated financial statement, or to dwell in great detail on the pros and cons of the volumes of arguments and Congressional studies over the whys and hows of determining charges and payments for mail transportation. However, there are some facts of absorbing interest that are vital to every citizen who helps to pay this bill—which means all of us.

It begins with the fact that approximately one sixth of all of the expenses of the Postal Service today (550 million dollars plus annually) is paid to carriers for transportation of the mail.

As the public's agent, the Post Office Department is the largest buyer of transportation in the world, and yet, under the laws as they stand, it holds very little control over the rate of expenditures for this service. Other Government agencies are involved in fixing rates for rail and air transportation, and total expenditures are set. At the same time, postage rates charged the public are subjected to pressures almost unbelievable to those outside of their influence.

Here is an example:

In February, 1960, domestic parcel-post rates were increased 17 per cent on the average. The Post Office Department bore the brunt of a public outburst of criticism across the country. Ironically the Department had no control over the increase since this particular service is required by law to substantially cover its costs. In 1958 Congress had raised postal-employee wages 10 per cent. It had required the inclusion of employee retirement costs of 6½ per cent in computing postage rates. The Interstate Commerce Commission had granted substantial increases in transportation rates for mail to all of the railroads in the country. It was perfectly clear to all who were familiar with the facts that rates must be raised to comply with the law.

The law, however, requires that all increases in parcel-post rates must first be approved by the Interstate Commerce Commission. It took a full year to obtain this approval because of the tactics of private groups who fought the increases every step of the way with every means at their command.

In the meantime, losses on parcel post alone caused more

than 80 million dollars to be added to other postal deficits due to insufficient rates, and accordingly charged back against the public in the form of costs that had to be made up by the Treasury from tax collections or borrowings.

The historic American position has been that the Government shall buy all possible services from private enterprise, and insofar as possible stay out of competitive business. The postal service in fact has been the leader in establishing and following this practice.

Thus mail contracts have helped immensely in the development of each of the great industries that by manufacture of equipment or operation of it make up the transportation business of the United States. We are proud of that record, which is so great that it overshadows all debate as to means and detail, past or present.

Sometimes, however, heated debate over this or that has thrown out of all perspective the true meaning of the Postal Service to American transportation.

For instance, the glamour of air traffic sometimes overshadows the great role that the Postal Service plays in supporting rail traffic. A few years ago debates over payment of so-called mail subsidies to steamships and to airlines, gave an impression of their size out of all proportion to the services in relation to the whole.

In our Administration, the Post Office Department has finally swept its costs clear of the "subsidy" problem through recent determination by the Congress that subsidy payments to airlines, ordered by the Civil Aeronautics Board, should be separated from the compensation for airmail transportation.

However, the Post Office still has to fight constantly the belief held by some people that its function is to underwrite transportation. We cannot do that and be fair to the taxpayer.

We are the trustees of the taxpayers in paying the bills, and part of our responsibility is to keep clear this perspective while the Congress appropriates money for the rates established by other agencies—by the Interstate Commerce Commission for rail transportation, and the Civil Aeronautics Board for air.

Railroad Mail: One of the worst falsehoods planted in the American mind by propaganda or ignorance is the feeling that the Post Office Department is "hurting" the railroads by its encouragement of air and highway mail transportation.

The truth is that in the year of this writing the railroads are being *paid more dollars than ever before for carrying mail.*

While rail service is shrinking, we not only are continuing to use the railroads to the fullest practical extent, but our modern transportation division actually is teaching and encouraging the railroads to provide new services for the postal operation that are economical for us and profitable for them.

To us railroad mail service is indispensable, and must be the backbone of our transportation structure. The railroads know this, as we know it, and the whole subject would be easier to handle if the public could understand it.

More than three fifths of all postal transportation dollars go to the railroads—342.2 million dollars out of our total transportation bill of 553.2 million dollars at this writing.

All of the other money we are spending in 1960 for transportation of the mail comes to 209 million dollars including everything from jet planes to the hire of small trucks for local transfers.

Two other easily understandable statistics complete this point:

> Between 1920 and 1959, the number of mail-carrying passenger trains declined from 10,000 to only 2,200—including all services everywhere in the United States, a drop of 78 per cent.
> From 1925 to 1959, the operating miles of passenger

trains dropped from 225,000 to 107,000, a drop of 52 per cent.

The railroads are the primary carriers of bulk mail—the second class consisting of periodicals and publications, much of the third-class or business advertising, and virtually all parcel post for intermediate or long distances. They carry practically all first-class transcontinental mail and most of the intermediate-range first-class mail.

Trains on longer runs are faster than highway transport, and the differential in charges as between airmail and first-class mail continues to give them a growing rather than shrinking opportunity in the field of handling letters.

In our goal of next-day delivery for all first-class mail in the United States, trains have special values in the runs of between 200 and 350 miles, if schedules are filled at night. And herein lies a field of development to which we have paid particular attention as it promises to be one of the great forward steps in postal transportation, revolutionizing older methods.

There is, in this connection, one weakness in the rail transport of mail that has come with the diminishing service of passenger trains so that these no longer run generally at all hours over all routes. The simple fact is that railroad passengers—people for whom the trains operate more and more as a specialized and limited service—do not necessarily ride at the best hours for handling of the mail.

Too often passenger trains in the remaining services run in daytime, morning or evening hours. They are timed to give passengers on shorter runs—as on the crowded trains between New York and Washington—the maximum possible business hours in one city and yet get them "home in time for bed" in the other.

For the mail service, however, this kind of scheduling is wasteful in time.

194

We have learned in our Post Office studies that next-day delivery is actually possible all over the United States, upon one condition: that is, that the great bulk of the mail moves between the hours of midnight and 6:00 A.M. This gives time for collection of the mail in late afternoon, and rapid despatch to other cities on carriers leaving around midnight. Arrival of mail in any city by 6:00 A.M. permits its sorting by modern methods and delivery on the day of receipt.

In this pattern, the railroads have a highly specialized place for the bulk of first-class mail traveling between 200 and around 350 miles. If the trains run in the midnight to 6:00 A.M. period, their service is for all practical purposes as effective as and far cheaper than air or highway mail carried the same distance. Also, above the 175-mile range of trucks or 250-mile range of buses there is virtually no competition because safety requirements hold down the six-hour travel rate of trucks or buses.

Thus the railroads have a large field as yet undeveloped in this special area of hauling first-class mail, while retaining the bulk of the parcel-post shipments and a good percentage of their own current business.

We have co-operated with the railroads in developing this special and profitable service, urging them to operate more "head-end trains," or those operating on express schedule in the early morning hours, without either passenger or freight cars, and solely as mail and express trains. Progress is being made in this direction.

The Pennsylvania Railroad took a bold new step in co-operating with our planning in April of 1959 when it completely reorganized service between New York and Washington, with results that already have shown a profit to the road and—happy thought in this time of rising costs—savings in costs of transportation of the mail. This road placed in service for the first time three special mail and express trains, operat-

195

ing on fast schedules to suit postal needs. At the same time it revised the assignment of Railway Post Offices to other passenger trains.

But there were dark spots, too, in the railway-mail picture, despite revisions in rates by the Interstate Commerce Commission which granted increases to the railroads amounting in 1958 and 1959 to 55 million dollars a year.

The Boston and Maine curtailed drastically its remaining passenger trains in New England, the Monon withdrew all passenger service between Indianapolis and Chicago, and the Lehigh System applied for authority to discontinue all passenger trains on its system.

But the rail service is neither dead nor dying. It needs, however, to move energetically with the times. In our section dealing with highway mail transportation, there are some excellent examples of how the railroads, working with the Postal Service, are moving to co-operate with highway mails, and thereby benefiting themselves.

Air mail: The revolutionary growth of airmail from the pioneering days to the "jet age" formed the subject of a preceding chapter. Here all that is necessary is a summary of the services and costs in order to give perspective to the transportation picture.

In 1960 the total domestic airmail operation of the United States is costing approximately 45 million dollars of public funds in return for the great network of airways serving every section of the country. This money represents fair payment for services, stripped of subsidies that once characterized airmail-contract payments.

In addition, 3.3 million dollars has been earmarked as compensation for those air routes over which airlift mail is handled.

The foreign airmail services that link the United States with

196

every other region of the world cost about 43 million dollars. However, this total includes 19 million dollars for the handling of military mail, for which the Post Office Department is reimbursed by the military branches of the Government.

The military mail of the United States incidentally has become one of the world's larger postal services all in itself. We currently have abroad, and presumably for the foreseeable future will continue to have, about 2.5 million Americans, including military and diplomatic personnel and their families. This relatively small number of persons all require an extended mail service covering great distances and vast areas.

The military mail service is operated by the armed forces, with the co-operation of the Post Office Department in main distribution of the mail, and under the supervision and with the training of our own staff members.

The postal service arranges for the transit to and from the United States of the military mail, which streams principally through the military post-office divisions established in the post offices at New York and San Francisco. Mail to Army and Air Force installations travels over fairly regular courses and schedules, but the Navy has worked for years, with extraordinary enterprise and efficiency, to solve its own peculiar problems of delivery of mail to units at sea.

It is common practice now for mail destined for a task force to be flown to a carrier in such a force at sea, from which distribution is made to the vessels in the immediate vicinity.

The height of ingenuity in "local delivery" to an isolated ship at sea was made in 1959 when, for the first time, a helicopter successfully dropped a bag of mail through the open hatch of a submarine that reached its conning tower just above the waves to receive this consignment.

Highway Mail: Highway mail has become a giant in public service because of development of the highways themselves and of the very efficient vehicles operating over them, and equally because the very development of highway hauling services has changed the pattern of railroad operation.

In 1925, when highways and vehicles were in an early stage of modern development, 60 per cent of the nation's communities had railway passenger and mail service. Today barely 30 per cent of these communities have passenger-train service.

The post office, therefore, has had to turn more and more to the highways, not only to meet minimum needs but also to reinforce the accelerated service program demanded by the public. In dollars this means that postal payments for highway transportation at this writing have passed the level of 95 million dollars a year. In planning and development, it has meant a revolution in procedures, still under way, but well advanced as the result of a complete national survey of mail transportation completed late in 1959.

In this work, and the job of compensating for critical shifts in transportation, we have much more to consider than simply the plight of the small cities and towns off the main lines. The very trunk lines themselves are undergoing great changes.

In 1959, as one example, when the Monon withdrew all of its passenger-train services between Indianapolis and Chicago, we had to set up new "star routes" immediately to provide a direct north-south trunk line for northern Indiana and western Michigan.

Drastic curtailment of passenger-train service in New England shut off essential Railway Post Office service and necessitated immediate replacement by Highway Post Offices. In many other instances, because of the almost overnight discontinuance of rail service, we had to establish temporary highway services and then reorganize them on a permanent basis.

Commuters and other railway users can see how the discontinuance of train service affects their personal lives. The same factors affect the postal service, but provide no acceptable excuse for delayed mail deliveries.

Thus we have had to meet crises in overland carriage of the mails by highway at the very time that the whole pattern of Star Route Services—the short-haul contract lines—were being revamped to make possible the next-day delivery of mail within the metropolitan areas.

Two main attacks were made on this problem of intercity highway mail carriage with, we think, exceptional success. One involved new extensions of the highway pattern and the other co-operation with the railroads to create more and better combination rail-highway services run by the railroads themselves.

On the highways we turned in 1959 to the use of passenger buses, which prior to that time had been used only in exceptional cases. There are now bus-mail contractors operating over wide areas of the United States, and in some cases the contracts cover entire bus systems. Thus we have a single contract with the Central Greyhound Lines for the carriage of first-class mail at a flat rate per bag over all of its routes operating in Minnesota, Iowa, Nebraska, Wyoming, Montana, North Dakota, South Dakota, Michigan, Wisconsin, Illinois and Manitoba, Canada. Thus history turns full circle and the modern "stagecoach" again becomes the carrier of the U.S. Mail.

In other areas where population centers are more scattered, where train service applicable to mail has diminished to the vanishing point, and where bus service is less frequent, fast-truck routes have been established on what might be termed the modern counterparts of the Pony Express.

A good example of this new type of express-truck run is in the "Four Corners" area where the states of Colorado, Utah, New Mexico and Arizona meet and where arid land that until recently was marked by only relatively small irrigated areas of sugar-beet country now supports a myriad of oil developments. This is truck-mail country of a special kind.

In the meantime, in densely populated areas we were forced to shift from trains to trucks with the decline of commuter services and consequently fewer train schedules, plus the need for overnight fast runs at the very hours when virtually no commuting trains are operated.

This was done in the Northern New Jersey Area, where 195 separate post offices form a single cluster in the next-day delivery pattern, and where the traditional train services, requiring truck pickup and delivery between post offices and railroad stations constituted a bottleneck. The entire traffic was shunted to trucks, thus establishing door-to-door post-office delivery service, at savings of hours in time, plus elimination of congestion during busy daytime hours.

But while the railroads have lost potential mail revenue in the face of these changes, our co-operative work with them has opened possibilities of new fields in co-ordinated highway-rail mail handling, run by the railroads and producing profitable business for them.

In May of 1959 the Chesapeake & Ohio placed in operation a new type of rail-highway vehicle named "Railvan," for regular operation as a mail and express carrier between Grand Rapids and Petosky, Michigan. It has dual retractable rail and highway wheels, running partly on the regular tracks and partly as an ordinary semitrailer on the highways.

The New York Central is experimenting at this writing with a vehicle called "Flexi-Van," which uses vans quickly transferable from highway vehicles to specially built rail cars. This type of vehicle recently completed its first year of satisfactory and profitable operation between Chicago and Detroit. The Central also has begun co-ordinated highway-rail mail deliveries between Albany and Buffalo in New York, and was exploring, in the spring of 1960, the possibility of operating a high-speed merchandise train with co-ordinated truck service between New York and Chicago.

All of this forecasts a period when the rail and highway lines, while competing among themselves, will come more and more into a unified pattern of efficient co-ordination in the postal service.

By Sea and Waterway: With all the dramatic developments in mail services in the past half century, we sometimes lose sight of the fact that there is not only a large foreign-mail steamship service, so stabilized as to be taken for granted, but that also a surprising number of Americans in the United States live either on islands or in areas that can be practicably served only by powerboats.

In this year, the United States has earmarked 11.2 million dollars for the cost of the ocean mails and—surprising to many of us—exactly a third that much to care for the postal needs of water-served residents ringing the country from Maine to the West Coast.

16

Bouncing Your Mail
Off the Moon

Sooner than you think the time is coming when a letter you deposit at your local post office, addressed to a point up to three thousand miles away, will be delivered in a matter of *hours*. And its privacy will be fully preserved all the way.

Moreover, your letter will not even have traveled in a straight line to its destination. It will, in fact, literally have taken a trip to the moon or to a man-made satellite!

The work toward this goal is well under way. We now regard as future "routine procedure" the transmission of letters—signed, sealed and delivered—by facsimile technique through the "bouncing" of microwave messages off the moon or a satellite.

This is no rare stunt. Already a single transmitting machine can thus send 180 pages per minute, three each second. A replica of the sealed letter placed in a small box in Washington or Battle Creek, Michigan, will be delivered sealed and with privacy fully assured with equal ease in New York or San Francisco.

Here is truly the "wave of the future." Here is speed incomparable to other means of transmitting messages set down on paper.

To start at the beginning of this story, we need only backtrack to 1959. This latest advancement of the dream of instantaneous communications involves not only a new means of serving the public interest but also perhaps an additional instrument of survival in the event of a new Armageddon.

Herein lies one of the finest examples of co-operation between the Post Office Department and other branches of government, and between government and private industry. It is comparable with, and perhaps as important as, those developments of weapons and space vehicles which must be cloaked in secrecy. It is a further example of the new determination of the postal service to seek the best in developing communication services for the public.

The project began with development by private research of the means of transmitting facsimiles of printed matter. In the 1930's various experimenters found that pictures could be transmitted over telephone wires and later over radio or television equipment—not just sent as television images are broadcast to receiving sets, but actually reproduced in picture form on pieces of paper.

As developed by the Department of Defense, the facsimile services using ordinary telephone wires were brought up to the point where twenty pages of material—twenty single-page letters—could be transmitted in an hour. Then as electronic development brought transmission work into the realm of microwaves or coaxial cables the speed of transmitters and receivers was increased to the rate of 10,800 pages per hour, or three per second instead of the former speed of *one each three minutes*.

The idea for facsimile mail goes back to a day early in 1959 when the Post Office Department was pondering what is perhaps the primary challenge facing this vast organization. The question was:

How can we break the economic and time barriers of a system requiring that privately recorded messages—small pieces of paper in essence containing writing and pictures—must be passed from hand to hand in every phase of delivery from the sender to the receiver?

In many other areas our society has moved to make more productive use of human resources.

The wheat fields of the Great Plains see billions of bushels of grain planted, tilled, harvested, and threshed by machines needing minimum human guidance. Even the problem of picking cotton mechanically has been solved. In transportation small teams of men direct the machines that carry hundreds of persons over land and sea or through the air, where little more than a century ago two men served a stagecoach carrying half a dozen.

It is true that in transport of the mail great strides have been made, but still not comparable with those in many other fields. In the handling of mail volume we have multiplied, prior to 1959, the capacities of individuals to handle mail by perhaps ten, through faster transportation and new mechanization. In 1890 the postal service of the United States required about 300,000 employees to handle 4 billion pieces of mail; in 1959, after seventy years of technological development that brought into being motorized highway transport and air transport, plus speed-ups of great magnitude in every other phase of communication, we required 550,000 pairs of hands to distribute a little over 60 billion pieces. In other words, nearly twice the personnel to handle fifteen times the number of pieces of mail.

In that seventy-year period costs jumped from slightly more than 66 million dollars in 1890 to more than 3.6 billion dollars in 1959. To curb further astronomical cost increases, manual handling of the ever-growing mail volume could not be continued. To do so would be a disgraceful lag, I think, in our age of development of techniques of mass production and mass handling, and this realization stimulated the imagination that our team brought to this problem.

Our reasoning took an interesting turn which I hope may inspire other similar ventures in the future. It ran something like this:

Many agencies of our Government, particularly the military, are spending billions of dollars annually on experiments in techniques and machines for communications primarily designed for security, which means either to prevent or if necessary to wage war successfully. For years, the military had been improving devices for the speedy transmission of vital messages, maps, and secret plans. Private research allied to this work had revolutionized many types of services, and the public had seen developments for commercial usage such as television growing up almost overnight.

In much of this work, the Post Office Department had participated as a "customer," but it had stood on the side lines. It had come into the picture of development of each new mode of transportation from stagecoach to jet airplane as a contractor, not as a developer. Yet the Post Office holds the unique spot of being the only government operation that provides a "customer service" through operation of nationwide facilities. Had not the "customer," as agent for every individual, the right and the responsibility to step out and develop or adopt the work of its fellow agencies for public service,

205

in contradistinction to sitting back and waiting for the crumbs
of improvement to fall from the tables of other agencies? Was
that fair to the public, or fair to itself?

There was no conflict or argument within the Government,
either at the Cabinet level or between subdivisions of the Departments at experimental and working levels. But we were
challenged to live up to our dreams.

We borrowed equipment then in use elsewhere, and one
day my office was the scene of what may well become a most
significant milestone in postal history.

Gathered there were representatives of the military services,
the F.B.I., C.I.A. and a handful of our own people. I described
the project we had in mind, and then handed to a messenger a
circular with name and description of a "wanted" criminal.
He took the circular to equipment located nearby and returned after a few minutes with a copy of it. The copy represented the end of an operation in which the circular had been
sent by facsimile equipment to Los Angeles and then re-
transmitted to Washington. As one of our enthusiasts remarked, "We are in business."

But the first step left many gaps to be filled:

(1) The speed of three sheets a minute was too slow and
prohibitively expensive;

(2) The material was not safeguarded by privacy, but was
open for inspection by anyone at either the sending or receiving end—a condition acceptable under the controls of military
security where carefully chosen personnel could be assigned,
but not for public use;

(3) Even the operation itself as a government-owned public service would run counter to rules and rights governing
privately owned communication agencies.

Step by step in a crash program the issues were resolved:

(1) Microwave transmission would answer the need for
speed and hence economy—if it could be developed as a mass

service. As you may know, microwaves are infinitesimally short radio waves with unlimited range, and like the waves that carry TV, FM radio, and radar—all in the longer wave lengths—they do not bend over the horizon; they travel only in a straight line.

(2) From the secret files of military research came ideas for the assurance of privacy—in effect, equipment that would receive sealed communications, unseal and transmit them, and deliver a sealed envelope at the receiving end;

(3) We determined to initiate this system with experimental work and backing, then to turn to the established private communications companies as our agents for development help and service, just as we let contracts for other types of mail carriage.

The first series of tests, conducted in special laboratories in Washington and other strategically located cities, indicated a high degree of adaptability of equipment already in production to the peculiar needs of the Post Office Department. Leading companies in the field of electronic communications lent some of their best experts to the experiment. In the joint venture were Western Union, American Telephone & Telegraph, Radio Corporation of America, Stewart-Warner, and A. B. Dick.

Government agencies provided testing material, and thousands of interagency messages were sent between the nation's capital, San Francisco, Los Angeles, Detroit, and Battle Creek. Included in the live-testing program were regular letters, official reports, maps, graphs, blueprints, charts, photographs, fingerprints, and contracts.

Coincidentally surveys were made as to availability of commercial facilities, should the experiments prove satisfactory. We found that mail transmission could be handled to a large extent at times when the commercial cables and relay systems are otherwise idle.

207

Our tests proved that we could expect a high quality of transmission, speed, and reliable performance, with relatively minor further development—that is, we found this to be so on paper. Equally important, we learned that the equipment could be developed in compact form to meet space requirements of many existing post offices.

By January, 1960, we were ready to proceed with the second phase of this operation—the actual award of a contract for production of equipment meeting all these requirements to the International Telephone and Telegraph Company. This contract covered the complete "package," and before winter ended, was well under way. We moved simultaneously toward many goals:

(1) Complete system engineering for high-speed transmission and facsimile transmission of mail at each of two major post offices.

(2) Engineering of the scanning and printing machines.

(3) Engineering of equipment to assure privacy.

(4) Engineering and production of prototype equipment for electronic switching and coding and related engineering for modification of electronic storage equipment.

(5) Purchase of necessary scanners, printers, openers, paper cutters, inserters, sealers, and tape-storage machines for both high-speed and medium-speed operations.

(6) Installation and testing of systems and equipment at key post offices.

(7) Completion of comprehensive reports covering the reliability and performance of systems and equipment, all economic and operational factors, and recommendations for development of the best possible national speed-mail system.

In a matter of months this entire project was completed and the first equipment was operating. As yet, in 1960, the transmissions were confined to government documents and mail. But "bouncing mail off the moon" was a new factor in our postal communications system.

Inevitably the day would come when the general public would have this service, at postage rates little if any higher than previously existed. Mail moving the length and breadth of the United States would be delivered within a few hours of its deposit, and almost all of this short span would represent the time needed for collection at one end and delivery to the exact address at the other.

The Post Office Department had made a contribution of magnitude to the future economic life of the United States. One also is tempted to wonder whether, on some day at an hour and a minute that cannot be foreseen, this revolutionary development may not be an ultimate link in the warning system protecting our security itself.

17

The People of the Postal Service

During the first week of my administration, Raymond V. McNamara and Charles Puskar paid a call upon me at my office.

Postmaster McNamara of Haverhill, Massachusetts, and Postmaster Puskar of Imperial, Pennsylvania, were president and secretary-treasurer, respectively, of the National Association of Postmasters. Mr. McNamara, incidentally, is a third-generation postmaster.

The main purpose of their visit, they told me, was to assure me of the full support of their membership behind our just-announced determination to modernize the service. It was a heartening experience and one I was to remember often in the years ahead; for no pledge of support ever was more genuinely kept than the one given to me that day.

The Association and its individual members rendered powerful assistance in every major step we took to provide better service for the American people. After Mr. McNamara's term of office, the same spirit prevailed throughout the presidencies of Postmasters John Fixa of San Francisco, Edward Baker of Detroit, and Hobart Wehking of Cincinnati.

Soon after the visit of Messers. McNamara and Puskar other employee organizations—notably the National League of Postmasters, the National Association of Postal Supervisors, the National Rural Letter Carriers' Association and the National Federation of Post Office Motor Vehicle Employees—talked with me of our plans and pledged their co-operation. In the ensuing years, these organizations, particularly during the leadership of Lowell K. Galbreth, Michael Nave, John B. Swigert, Warren B. Bledsoe and Paul M. Castiglioni, spelled out that co-operation with helpful and effective work of untold value to our program. More recently, the National Federation of Post Office Clerks, under the leadership of J. Cline House, have co-operated with us in the efforts to modernize the postal service.

Despite the fact some of the postal employee groups are led by labor leaders whose actions at times seem contrary to the best interests of their members, the response to our efforts throughout the great ranks of postal employees was cause for real inspiration. In the National Association of Postal Supervisors the feeling was so strong that this influential group withdrew their affiliation with the AFL-CIO. Representing a complete cross section of our citizenry over the length and breadth of the land, the dominant spirit of the half-million postal employees was not only a willingness but an eagerness to participate in progress.

Especially in the light of that spirit, it was of first impor-

U.S. MAIL

tance that we set about to modernize not only the postal facilities, but personnel practice as well.

The sprawling postal operation in 1953 had no training program, either for aiding workers to increase their efficiency and opportunities or to serve as a basis for the assessment of work values.

With no safety program, the Post Office Department had what was called a "disgraceful" accident record. There was no selection method for the promotion of efficient employees, and no effective job grading, and thus little incentive and unfair pay scales.

There was no public information service worth the name.

It was understandable, under these circumstances, why morale was low, and why there was a high turnover in employment.

It was necessary, also, to bridge a large gap separating the Post Office management and the leadership of the sixteen postal employee unions, with the latter naturally keeping a wary eye on the change in Administration which brought into office a political party that the bulk of organized labor had been encouraged by its politically minded spokesmen to consider as "the other camp."

These postal unions were: National Association of Postmasters of the United States; National League of Postmasters; National Association of Postal Supervisors; National Association of Letter Carriers; National Rural Letter Carriers' Association; United National Association of Post Office Clerks; National Federation of Post Office Clerks (A.F.L.); National Alliance of Postal Employees; National Federation of Post Office Motor Vehicle Employees; The National Association of Special Delivery Messengers; National Federation of Federal Employees; American Federation of Government Employees; National Postal Transport Association; National Association of Post Office and Surface Postal Transport Mail Handlers,

212

Watchmen and Messengers (AFL); National Star Route Mail
Carriers' Association; National Association of Post Office and
General Services Maintenance Employees.

When I took office, I was amazed to find how little emphasis was being placed on personnel administration. The records
did not indicate exactly how many employees the Post Office
Department had, but I understood the number then was in
excess of four hundred thousand.

On checking further, I learned, as I had expected, that some
70 per cent of the Department's entire appropriations was
being spent for personnel services. I felt there could hardly
be a more important job on my staff than heading up the personnel division.

It was not altogether a simple administrative thing to give
this position the standing it required. The prerogatives of
Congress being what they are, it was necessary for me to request legislation authorizing an additional Assistant Postmaster General to direct the personnel function. My purpose,
of course, was to make this function of equal rank with Assistant Postmasters General responsible for Operations, Finance, etc. The legislation was passed and Mr. Eugene J.
Lyons was appointed soon after.

I was to learn, to my surprise, that this was a "first" in the
Government—that no other agency had ranked the civilian
personnel administration function at the Assistant Secretary
level. By comparison, private industry for many years had considered the function important enough so that most of the
major, progressive companies had vice presidents in charge of
personnel administration or labor relations.

The people of the postal service concerned me first of all,
and I knew that the experienced management men on my new
top staff felt the same way. No policy guide in any area meant
more to me than the one I gave to the new Assistant Post-

master General in charge of personnel; and, as I had felt sure would be the case, it was very capably carried out. It stated, simply:

> We must strive to gain insight into the human factor which plays such a large role in the effectiveness of the postal service and accept personnel policies which recognize the importance and dignity of the individual.

With this guideline went the authority to develop a complete program of positive action.

It is essential to understand that few, if any, of the major postal reforms of the last seven years, whether in public service or for the benefit of Post Office personnel, could have come about without the presence of that hardy spirit of service we have noted.

The postal corps, given the opportunity, has shown all the latent strength of its tradition—a tradition signally honored in 1959 when both President Eisenhower and Vice President Nixon joined with me in paying our tribute to this spirit at the fifty-fifth annual meeting of the National Association of Postmasters of the United States.

Our postmasters are the individuals on whom so much must depend in an organization in which local management on a vast scale is of key importance.

The personnel scope of the postal system is sometimes compared with that of General Motors Corporation, the largest private company in the United States and one which in the year 1959 employed about the same number of persons in its many diverse manufacturing and sales operations. But the comparison is not wholly accurate in one essential respect.

Our service and this industrial company span almost the entire range of skills, although in differing types and degrees, but even General Motors has heavily concentrated areas of

214

employment; also it meets the public only through its dealer organizations.

The postal service is literally everywhere; postal workers are in every community, no matter how small, and they are members of every community—often leading members. They thrive, as they should, on local initiative and pride.

Just as we have taken the local post offices out of purely political domination, so we have tried by every practicable means to take local personnel management out of Washington, and to give the postal service employee proper supervision, opportunity, and appreciation where he works.

We have taken a new co-operative approach to the representatives of the postal workers' own unions and associations by appointment of a Special Assistant for Employee Relations to work in Washington on the full-time job of dealing with union representatives, providing information on policy development, handling complaints and grievances, and taking positive action to correct deficiencies.

This system has been extended throughout the field, with comparable activity in each of the fifteen administrative regions.

Coincidentally, postal policies and instructions were co-ordinated in revised, easy-to-understand publications and the Postal Service News was transformed early in 1959 into an information organ for the Bureau of Personnel. Now we can talk to each other.

However, communications are effective only when there is something tangible to communicate. In the years prior to the writing of this work we have seen the tangibles take definite form and outline, all the way from training to adequate compensation and incentive bonuses.

In 1959 a procurement officer of the Postal Service, for using creative imagination, won one of the largest incentive bonuses ever paid by the service. His award was $1,200. He did not invent a new electronic machine or take a rocket mailplane to the moon. Rather, he dramatized the meaning of everyday development of money-saving ideas. He designed a folding stand to hold temporary cardboard cases used in sorting the excessive mail loads at Christmas.

Every post office in the United States is plagued by the need for such equipment in periods of great volume, and the makeshift manner of meeting the needs has caused untold loss and waste. The stand that won the award packs away in its own shipping container, a little over 6 feet long and 27 inches wide and only 5 inches thick. It can be assembled in less than a minute.

Incentive awards—so long commonplace in private industry—have skyrocketed developments of new ideas in the postal service. The year 1959 saw useful suggestions increase half again over those submitted in 1958, which was itself the fourth year of the expanded program. After all, where is there a better place to look for new ideas to meet the pressures upon us than in the ranks of the individuals who wrestle with the day-by-day problems?

There is, however, much more to incentive and development of economical efficiency than the rare incentive award.

In 1956 we began the challenging task of surveying postal needs and giving appropriate recognition in pay to those doing the job. Personnel specialists collaborated with operating officials in describing and ranking new standard positions required by radical changes in the postal field service, installing new postal systems and mechanized equipment, and revising procedures and methods. It became evident that we could not operate a jet-age postal service with horse-and-buggy procedures.

As one result of this work, 1,760 postmasters in 1959 received different salary ratings on the basis of local changes in financial and service responsibilities. Corresponding adjustments were made for their principal subordinate supervisors. Other revisions were made throughout the levels of second- and third-class postmasterships.

And while we established rules for fair compensation of those already in the service, new teams were sent into the field—seventy-six of them—to assure the quality of individuals selected for initial employment or promotion.

These boards went out, as so many business teams must do today, to look for quality among applicants rather than quantity. They have shown excellent results in the consistently high caliber of people coming to work with us, particularly in the larger industrial cities. Getting the right person for a job, and then making it attractive to him, is half the economy battle, for little else is as wasteful as high turnover in employment.

When I mention "him" in the employment picture, a heavy qualification is needed, for never before has the postal service put more emphasis on the "her" in recruiting career workers. This is an essential part of our aggressive recruiting program.

Traditionally women have been employed in the service in limited numbers, primarily in small towns where men have not been avaliable. In the larger cities, postal positions have been filled almost entirely by men. In fact, the small number of women hired seemed to reflect an unwarranted discrimination. We have opened the door to careers in which women now are welcome on the basis of unprejudiced competition and co-operation.

Meanwhile, within the service, a whole new machinery has been established to train and reward those ambitious to get ahead, including the new fields opened up by introduction of complex equipment. In the year preceding this writing, forty-three thousand employees took examinations to qualify for promotions in the management, technical, mechanical, and clerical fields, while five hundred took the technical tests for the positions of Methods and Standards Officers.

Training officers have worked closely with engineers and other staff officials to supply technical guidance in orientation and on-the-job skills developed for employees, as new machines and methods have been installed.

The safety program has made tremendous strides toward eliminating costly accidents. Motor-vehicle accidents have been drastically reduced to the lowest figure in the history of the Department at a savings of hundreds of thousands of dollars. For the fourth consecutive year the Department won the National Safety Council Traffic Safety Citation for its outstanding example in guiding postal personnel to full local and national support of the Council's "Back the Attack on Traffic Accidents Campaign."

Aggressive action has been taken also to prevent industrial accidents, and the number of lost-time accidents has been sharply reduced.

The Department in 1960 is at a peak of personnel relations —mutual understanding and co-operation between officials and staff. Positive steps have been taken to expand and improve employee-management contacts, to adjust each phase of the personnel program to the new methods of moving the mail, and to emphasize quality in the selection of employees for essential positions.

Insofar as is possible, we have worked to make this service one of opportunity. We believe this has been accomplished.

18

The Post-Office Dollar

There is an awesome responsibility involved in an assignment to spend other people's money wisely. If an individual lets a portion of his means dribble carelessly through
his fingers, it affects only one or relatively a few persons. But
waste in a business or public agency is waste of many people's
money and can easily multiply into stupendous figures.

Probably few businesses have the problem the Post Office
Department has in watching its money, and handling it carefully—in this business where revenues come mainly from sales
measured in pennies, while expenditures in most categories of
cost mount into scores of millions of dollars.

Consider the billions of daily transactions involved in the

sale of stamps alone, and the details requiring attention in the handling of more than a million money orders on the average every working day.

And we have side lines of merchandise and services built up by custom such as selling U. S. Savings Bonds, Documentary Internal Revenue Stamps, and Migratory Bird Hunting Stamps —for all of which we are reimbursed, but which bring added duties. In the service category our rural letter carriers survey wild-fowl populations, report forest fires, and distribute livestock and crop-acreage survey cards.

The Post Office delivers flags for funerals of deceased war veterans, conducts examinations for civil service applicants, locates relatives of deceased personnel for the Armed Forces, gives applicants blanks for alien registration and receives all of their annual registrations in January of each year, certifies widows and children for various government benefits, and supplies blank income-tax forms for its patrons. To the exent that the Department does not receive reimbursement in these cases, it may be noted that any costs are more than offset by services performed free for the postal service by other Government agencies.

These functions add to the complexities of our operations, but of course they are small items relative to our main job. In considering the business-management problems, we repeat that we have a staff of more than a half million persons operating in about thirty-five thousand post offices, handling more than 61 billion pieces of mail a year.

One would take it for granted that the budgeting, auditing and accounting procedures for such a business would necessarily be among the most efficient in our country.

But I was shocked to find, in 1953, that the Post Office was operating under many rules and practices last overhauled in 1908.

The postal service was running a deficit of 2 million dollars a day, without knowing whether these expenditures were producing adequate results. A year might elapse between expenditure of money and final accounting that gave any idea of the true financial status of affairs. Even then, the picture was hardly complete; the balance sheet covered cash items only and did not show the value of the postal investment in property, plant, and equipment.

Each of forty thousand postmasters handled his own accounting and when their separate reports reached Washington, they were forwarded directly on to Asheville, North Carolina, to a section of the General Accounting Office. There checks were made for honesty, but no machinery existed to test efficiency.

Costs of subsidies to airlines and the cost of carrying official penalty and franked mail for the entire government was borne by the Department. Financial statements were considered more as historical documents than aids to management. Accounting, budgeting, and costing were performed by each of the various Bureaus with little co-ordination between them.

Much too little was being done in the way of an adequate internal audit program to protect the assets of the Government and appraise the Department's fiscal management policies. There were too few professionally trained accountants and internal auditors on the job.

If these statements appear to be critical, they are not presented as criticism of any people, but of the kind of seriously inefficient system that can evolve in a government service if sound policies are not firmly followed—inefficiencies often obscured to the public but costing that same public dearly in tax funds and ultimately, if not repaired, in the basic strength of the government itself.

In the following chapter I will take up another kind of gross inadequacy which still exists *today* in the operation of the postal service—one, I would add, with which American taxpayers have every reason to be deeply concerned.

The foregoing notes on the earlier fiscal situation in the Post Office Department are in the nature of background observations—not personal observations alone, but findings reported in some degree by the first Hoover Commission and the Comptroller General of the United States.

In a report to the House Committee on Post Office and Civil Service, the Comptroller General said, in part:

> . . . the Department's accounting fails to meet any of the requirements normally expected of a modern accounting system except that it serves to establish accountability for cash. It does not provide for control of other assets for which it is responsible; it does not furnish management with the financial information it needs; nor does it fully disclose the Department's financial condition or the results of its operations.

The Comptroller General criticized: (1) lack of understanding of the manner in which accounting could be used as a tool of management; (2) absence of professionally qualified accounting personnel; (3) failure to assign adequate staff to accounting responsibilities; and (4) a general inertia and resistance to change, including a reluctance to accept any advice or suggestions from qualified outsiders.

The Congress had passed legislation in 1951 on part of the Hoover Commission reports, authorizing the Department to set up its own system of accounting and internal controls, which started with the establishment of twelve regional accounting offices. However, modernization of the postal service, as we saw it, had to proceed on many fronts simultaneously, and each activity was necessarily a part of the whole concept of adequate business management.

The first important step was to take a financial management inventory—of fiscal policy, personnel, machinery, technique, and functions. Extensive surveys were made of accounting practices and procedures in the Department Headquarters. Other surveys were made in typical field installations.

The problems disclosed by the surveys focused attention on the need for a complete overhauling and modernization of all financial and accounting activities. This pattern had long been developed in industry. A modern industrial type controllership was needed, including:

Modernization of the entire accounting system of the postal establishment.

Integration of all accounting, auditing, budgetary, fiscal, and cost operations.

Timely financial statements and reports.

Measurement of activities so that the Department could perform at its maximum capabilities and develop a scientific approach to efficiency improvement.

Financial control of the assets of the postal establishment.

Interpretation of the influence of outside business and economic factors.

Objective guidance to all levels of management.

Simplification of accounting procedures and reporting by streamlining to the maximum extent possible.

Establishment of realistic management targets and procedures for measuring conformity.

Establishment of a modern paper-work management program.

The accounting firm of Alexander Grant and Company was engaged to help us accomplish these goals. The Comptroller General assisted by assigning an able systems staff to the Post Office Department. Under the guidance of these two groups, the employees of the postal service carried forward the modernization of the Department's financial and accounting program.

In the three years between 1953 and 1956, with concentrated effort in all areas, the financial management picture was completely changed.

Seldom in financial history, I am sure, has a change of such scope occurred in an enterprise of this magnitude—private or public. In his report of January 16, 1956, the Comptroller General stated;

> The modernization of financial and accounting practices in the Department is one of the most extensive ever undertaken in a single sweep in the Government and is now well under way. . . . We believe the Department should be commended for the realistic and aggressive manner in which it has pursued this problem.

A streamlined system of accounting and financial reporting, equal to modern business practice, had been installed. The former diffusion of financial management of functions had been corrected and an up-to-date controllership organization was created which consolidates responsibility of all financial management functions. Trained personnel have been carefully recruited from business and government to staff the supervisory positions, thus assuring continuance of this program. There are fifty-six certified public accountants in the postal organization.

To provide regional management with effective tools for decision-making and to relieve postmasters of functions unrelated to their primary duties, fifteen regional controller officers had been established to serve the regional directors and their staffs.

Accounting procedures were completely reorganized under a concept that uses the latest types of mechanical and electronic equipment to develop the facts and promptly report them, and then, through intelligent analysis and interpretations, gives the entire postal management at all levels an effective tool in the control of costs.

These accounting and financial changes have resulted in savings of more than 15 million dollars a year.

I now receive at my desk every month within three weeks after the end of the prior month a complete set of operating and financial statements, including a balance sheet, covering the entire postal establishment. An accrual accounting system has been established in conformance with modern industrial practices. A complete inventory of our tangible property, aggregating $1 billion, has been taken and is being placed on the books.

The years that have passed since installation of these methods have seen the effective "revolution" in the postal service, as it has developed (insofar as remaining limitations permit) into a true public "business."

Other chapters have dealt in detail with improvements in the postal service through mechanized post offices and early work in microwave transmission, but many of these developments depended upon the invigorating effect of a sound fiscal policy.

Such developments would include these:

In 1959, 110 post offices were added to the list of areas receiving city delivery service, thus giving this service to more than 100,000 additional families and 26,000 business firms; 1,051,000 families and 100,000 business firms were added at existing city delivery offices. Also 3,150 mailsters (midget cars for city route carriers) were assigned to 188 city delivery offices. Studies at representative offices using mailsters indicate the original cost of mailsters is recovered in approximately 2.2 years.

We reduced requirements for extending rural delivery service from three to two families per mile. This action has benefited 441,304 families, or approximately 1,500,000 persons.

Our total of new buildings, privately constructed and leased for post offices, passed the 3,500 mark.

Approximately 3,000 *existing* leased buildings will be furnished with modern equipment in the modernization program now under way, and approximately 1,500 existing Federal buildings will be renovated, enlarged and equipped with modern fixtures over the next four years.

The United States Postal Service probably is the largest real estate firm in the world; it definitely has the biggest motor-vehicle fleet. Our government-owned motorized fleet in 1960 consisted of 39,000 standard commercial vehicles, 85 per cent of which are one-ton or less. Operating costs of the fleet have been reduced materially, due to greatly improved maintenance practices and closer supervision. Average cost of operation for the entire fleet is six cents per mile per vehicle. (This includes all vehicles, from ¼-ton mailsters through tractor-trailer rigs.) A short wheelbase, 4-cylinder engine truck, the Metro-Mite, has been thoroughly tested for city delivery use. Procurement is anticipated in 1960 on a number of these vehicles for more economic utilization in certain mail-delivery activities.

A comprehensive study of the entire postal transportation system, the first since 1921, was virtually completed at this writing. Initial objective of the study is to find economic and efficient ways to provide next-day delivery for first-class mail, whenever practicable, and to improve delivery for all other classes. In a broader sense, the study will serve as a guide for charting transportation planning and policy for at least the next five years.

Legislation was prepared for submission to the Congress in 1960 which would permit the Department to make agreements with air carriers for transportation of any class of mail (except airmail and air parcel post) without the requirement of costly, time-consuming mail-rate proceedings in each case. New sources of mail traffic which would become available to the carriers would effectively decrease subsidy requirements of subsidized carriers, such as local service carriers (106 million ton-miles of airmail and 17 million ton-miles of first-class mail were airlifted during the year.)

Regional controllers provided the data on the basis of which regional office teams now systematically visit each of the sixty largest post offices. They review and analyze operating results, in comparison with predetermined targets, and aid in developing solutions to manpower utilization problems. Similar reporting and controls are being established for all offices with annual receipts over one million dollars, making a total of 275 offices receiving controllership-type analysis.

We continue to improve our skills in the regional controller offices. As a result, we have reduced by 100 the necessary employees in each of the regional controller offices.

After two years of negotiations and study, all air and rail carrier bills soon will be computed daily, then paid on either a seven-day or twenty-eight-day basis by each regional controller. Four years ago, we had two years of backlog in unsettled air and rail claims. Now, we will pay fourteen days after each week or twenty-eight-day period, whichever method the carriers elect. The simplified methods are very accurate, eliminating thousands of hours of clerical and operating peoples' time in locating errors.

If the postal system had tried to cope with the tremendous growth of our nation without this modernization program, the deficits incurred in its operation would have piled up into astronomical figures—literally billions of dollars more than the deficits actually experienced.

These latter have been far too great. They have also been unjustifiable. But no amount of modernization and improvement of accounting and budgeting policies, of programs for efficiency and economy, could possibly offset them. They result from the iron grip which the Congress, in the end, holds over the financial management of the Post Office Department. And in this lies a grave problem for every American to consider—a problem to which I feel I must devote a large part of the chapter which follows.

19

For the Future:
The Right to Manage

James A. Farley, for whom I have a high regard—as does
everyone, I think, who knows him—was Postmaster General of the United States from 1933 to 1940.

Shortly after I moved into the office in 1953, Mr. Farley came
to visit me and wish me well. Chatting, we strolled into the
long oak-paneled corridor which is adjacent to the office and
which contains a gallery of portraits of every Postmaster General from the beginning to the present. For some time we
moved slowly along the line of pictures, talking about the man
in each, including those by name of Farley and Summerfield
(whose likeness had just been hung that day); and as we returned to our starting point and paused in front of the picture

there, Mr. Farley stood bemused a moment and then put his arm about my shoulder and said, "You know, Arthur, when you study the record of this Department, you realize there have been only three great Postmasters General in the entire history of the country."

I looked up into the solemn face of six-foot-four "Big Jim" and replied, "Well, I guess that's possibly so, Jim. . . . Who's the other one?"

Without blinking, as he gazed at the portrait in front of him he said, "Benjamin Franklin."

I looked for a twinkle in his eye, but his sober countenance remained unchanged, as if he were utterly serious.

Later I recounted this episode at a luncheon which Mr. Farley and I were attending, and there he joined in the laughter. But I do not know to this day which two Postmasters General he was listing in company with Franklin—nor shall I ever divulge the pair I had in mind until he speaks first!

In any event, what I am trying to say here is that I hope the next Postmaster General will prove to be among the greatest of the long line. He will face a great challenge.

Whatever general course may be taken, I feel confident the administration which succeeds my own will want to sustain the major programs that are aimed at increasing postal efficiency through: mechanization of operations; modernization of facilities, including new post-office buildings and automatic services; sound fiscal and management policies; restoration of the postal operation to its historic capability of paying its own way; continued programs to attract well-qualified personnel and to assure for all postal employees opportunities and work satisfaction equal to the times; and continued development of better and faster ways to transport the mails in the future.

There must be persistent research and development, taking the fullest possible advantage of work done by other government branches in such revolutionary areas as electronic processes and facsimile transmission.

It is only honest to recognize that a development of the massive potenital of facsimile transmission may in time affect a major part of the mail-carrying business of the railroads, airlines, and highway transport. If such should be the case, very substantial problems for these great transportation media could of course be a result. But we in America have learned better, and more to our profit than perhaps any other people in the world, that it does not pay to hold back progress. Dislocations occur and must be adjusted, but in the end the economy and strength of the nation are advanced, to the benefit of all the people. Thus in the carrying of the mail the stagecoach could not stand in the way of the locomotive and the rail-running mail car was inevitably forced to yield part of its task to the speed of air transport.

In an age in which major advances in science may be marked almost daily, the postal service *must* be responsive to development and change or it will fall irretrievably behind the essential demands upon it.

Our population in 1960 is about 180 million. It is growing so rapidly that by 1985 it will be 250 million.

As our prosperity and education increase, our people will make greater use of the mails. As compared with an average of 350 pieces of mail per person in 1960, it seems clear that the total per person will double over the next twenty-five years to an annual average of 700 pieces per capita.

That will mean a total of 175 billion pieces of mail a year, or *almost three times the load in 1960.*

The preparations to meet these onrushing needs are effectively under way, but over and above these programs, an urgent problem hangs over the postal operation that gravely affects the outlook not only for the service but the economic welfare of the whole nation.

231

Drawing upon almost eight years of intense personal as well as official devotion to the problems of this great postal service, I must set down for study by my successors this series of frank conclusions:

The first is that the postal service can and must be placed on a basis of paying its own way.

The second is that it is unlikely to achieve this basis as long as it remains at the mercy of some members of the Congress who will use their power over it to suit their political ambitions and purposes.

The third is that the postal establishment must be put above the dictation of pressure groups determined that the Government shall continue contributing vast subsidies to their profit-making business operations.

The fourth is that, if the present political and pressure-group controls over postal operations are extended into the future, the Post Office Department will continue to be one of the largest annual contributors to our Federal debt.

And the fifth is that, if this great service is permitted instead to be master of its own house under reasonable balances and safeguards, it will grow magnificently as a proud and positive part of the economy the American taxpayer wants.

I wish every taxpayer could mark well and take to heart the following facts:

I have previously noted that in the period from 1946 to 1960 the postal deficit added up to some 6.8 billion dollars despite the application of major efficiencies to the operations after 1953. This deficit was almost *half* the total increase of 15 billion dollars in the Federal debt during this time!

Nor does this 6.8 billion dollars represent the total burden incurred. The nation's taxpayers are paying well over 200 million dollars' interest *each year* on the deficit.

The staggering postal losses which brought it about have been due solely to inflationary rises in costs of wages, transportation and supplies purchased by the Post Office, without compensating increases in revenues.

In short, the Congress has neglected to increase postage rates to meet the increased costs.

We can estimate that these added costs since just 1952 have run at 915 million dollars.

In the years from 1932 to 1959 costs of handling first-class mail increased by more than 100 per cent, while letter postage rates went up 33 per cent, or only one third as much. But that is far from all the story.

Most readers will be familiar with the system whereby our mail is carried largely in three classes. First class is generally letter mail. Second class is made up largely of magazines and newspapers. Third class is generally what is called direct-mail advertising, used very largely by business firms.

Because second- and third-class users have been paying highly favored rates, the Post Office losses on handling second-class mail in 1959 were running at nearly 300 million dollars a year; on third-class mail nearly 200 million dollars a year. The Government, in other words, was paying what amounted to nearly a half billion dollars a year in subsidies to these users!

With the great vision with which he has addressed himself to fiscal soundness for the future as well as the present, President Eisenhower has given earnest attention to our postal objectives. I have always found him highly sympathetic to the postal problems and extremely helpful in providing leadership toward their solution. He has consistently and firmly advocated more equitable postage rates to place the Post Office Department on a self-supporting basis.

Throughout the momentously full and demanding days of his two terms in office, he has never been too busy to discuss—in detail and with surprisingly keen knowledge of the subject—any matter affecting the postal service and its employees I have presented to him.

President Eisenhower has been forthright and fearless in op-
posing and even vetoing some pay-rate and other postal legislation which he felt either was discriminatory against some postal employee groups or was inimical to the best interests of all
the people. But it is a matter of record that no President in our
history ever demonstrated greater personal interest in the progress of the postal service and the people in its ranks.

He signed Public Law 68 which was unquestionably the
most realistic postal-salary reclassification of record. In 1958 the
President signed into law one of the highest postal-pay increases of all time.

In addition, no one worked more diligently than did President Eisenhower in obtaining Government Group Life Insurance, which was enacted into law by his signature on August
17, 1954. This protection has proven a blessing in countless
cases when tragedy has taken the breadwinner of the family;
and, of course, these benefits will continue to the welfare of
government employees.

The recently enacted Health Insurance Plan for Government
Employees, which became effective July 1, 1960, is another
project to which the President has been especially and personally dedicated.

In many ways and in a manner which has perhaps not been
generally observed, President Eisenhower has placed into mo-
tion many vital programs for the present and future enhance-
ment of government careers.

Now, why should the Postal Service pay its own way?

The Post Office is different from other departments of Government which perform services benefiting all the people. The
nature of those services is such that there is no way to measure
them person by person or, in most cases, to break them down
into measurable units. It is the proper role of taxation to assume
the burden of paying for such unmeasurable services provided

234

for the equal good of all citizens. But in the Post Office, services are performed in the form of individual transactions—all measurable, all distinguishable, each from the other.

When you put a letter in the mailbox, its handling by the Post Office is a measurable service for an identifiable user. When a magazine publisher puts a million copies of a heavy magazine into the mails, which have to be handled essentially just like your letter, that, too, is an exact service for an identifiable organization. The same is true of the user who asks the Post Office to deliver millions of pieces of direct-mail advertising.

That is why postal rates are charged. If we were to argue that huge annual postal losses should not concern us, we must ask why the Post Office should charge any fees at all. Why should it not carry every person's mail, every publisher's magazines and every advertiser's circulars free of charge and pass the whole cost on to the taxpayers?

The fact is that historically our Government has expressed itself as opposed to postal deficits because they result in passing off much of the cost of service from the large users to the taxpaying citizen.

One of the first acts of our Continental Congress in 1782 referred pointedly to "exacting such postage as may be requisite to defray the expenses of the post offices."

And suiting the action to the word, the Post Office in the first thirty years of operation under the postal policies of the Founding Fathers produced a revenue surplus of 15 per cent!

Over the years the Congress has many times reaffirmed the proposition that the Postal Service should pay its own way.

In 1950, in connection with the parcel-post system, Congress put it strongly with the provision that:

. . . hereafter, none of the funds appropriated to the Post Office Department from the general fund of the Treasury

shall be withdrawn from the Treasury until the Postmaster
General shall certify . . . to the establishment of such rate
increases or other reformations . . . as may be necessary
to insure the receipt of revenue . . . sufficient to pay the
cost of such service.

In 1958, Congress again wrote this policy into its legislation,
stating:

Postal rates and fees shall be adjusted from time to time as
may be required to produce the amount of revenue approximately equal to the total cost of operating the postal establishment. . . .

But what the Congress has written as policy and what it has
actually done in these postwar years are two widely different
things!

In the year after the 1950 declaration, the postal deficit ran to
some 564 million dollars, and in 1952 it rose to 719 million dollars.

Let us note again that in 1959, the year after that policy was
reasserted, the cost of handling second- and third-class mail
was some 500 million dollars over the revenue from that service; and that the total postal deficit in 1960 was expected to be
around 650 million dollars.

I would point out, too, that—fine policy intentions notwith-
standing—magazines that go into the second-class mails today
cost your Post Office an average of four cents apiece more to
handle than the sender pays for this service. Pieces of third-
class mail cost an average of one cent more. In the aggregate,
these extra costs mount to enormous figures.

Why does the Congress not enact postal rates that will "produce the amount of revenue approximately equal to the total
cost of operating the postal establishment"?

I know it is not because of any material opposition by the
average citizen who uses the first-class mail. If in 1960 the post-

age for a first-class letter were increased, as we have requested, from four cents to five cents an ounce (airmail from seven to eight cents), the difference would mean an average additional cost of one-half cent a day per family. In other words, the average family over a full year's time would pay about $1.80 more for postage than it was paying before. On the other hand, the lifting of the postal deficit burden from the cost of government, removing the great tax and inflationary pressures it otherwise generates, would certainly save the family more than $1.80 per year.

The real resistance to an equitable rate adjustment comes from some of the politically powerful users of the second- and third-class privileges who are determined to perpetuate the subsidies they enjoy. They particularly like the postal-type subsidy because in operation it does not come to them as an outright subsidy payment but rather in the form of Uncle Sam picking up the tab for a considerable part of their postal bill. Certain of the large magazine publishers therefore can go on criticizing outright government subsidies to other groups while they enjoy their own, sight unseen.

Essentially the same reason lies behind the powerful resistance put up by many direct-mail advertisers, largely through a battery of very vocal direct-mail associations and their Washington lobbyists.

The pressures exerted by these groups, especially upon important members who have great influence on some key committees in Congress, have been largely responsible for the failure of Congress to put postal services on the proper basis of payment as used.

This is not by any means intended to be a blanket indictment.

During the past seven and a half years I have worked very closely with many Members of the Congress. Two stalwart

Members of the House of Representatives, Congressman Tom Murray of Tennessee, and Congressman Edward H. Rees of Kansas, who have served as Chairman or Members of the House Post Office and Civil Service Committee during these years, have been of great help to us in all legislative matters affecting the ability of the Post Office Department to best serve the people. In this, they have been joined by some outstanding members of these committees, notably Congressmen Katherine St. George of New York, and August E. Johansen and Elford Cederberg of Michigan.

In the Senate, Senator Carl Hayden of Arizona, Chairman of the Senate Committee on Appropriations, and Senator A. Willis Robertson of Virginia, Chairman of the Senate Subcommittee of Appropriations, have given the utmost attention to our problems and noteworthy support to our efforts, as have Senators Roman L. Hruska of Nebraska; Thomas H. Kuchel of California and Gordon Allot of Colorado.

Effective support has come too, from the Republican leadership in the Congress; notably Senators Everett Dirksen of Illinois and Styles Bridges of New Hampshire and Congressmen Charles A. Halleck of Indiana; Joseph Martin of Massachusetts; Leslie Arends of Illinois and Gordon Canfield of New Jersey.

Five times President Eisenhower sent special and urgent requests to the Congress to enact postal-rate legislation in the interest of the country's taxpayers, but in each case, these requests were bottled up before some action finally was achieved in the postal-rate revision of 1958. Some members of the Congress have consistently yielded to pressures of powerful magazine publishers and third-class mail users to continue the subsidies that have cost hundreds of millions of dollars in government debts and taxes in the past fifteen years.

At the same time, these same members of Congress always have been among the first to vote increases in postal costs

238

while making no pretense whatsoever of finding any ways to provide the revenues to meet those costs.

It has been no small shock to me to see the manner in which the heads and representatives of some of the great magazine publishing firms have testified in rate hearings before committees of Congress.

In 1951, 1955 and 1957, they filled these hearings with dire predictions as to the effect on their circulations and, therefore, their volume of advertising, if any increase in postal rates was approved. The records show that the two rate increases enacted in 1952 and 1958 had no such effect. The annual volume of magazine advertising rose from around $500 million in 1950 to about $850 million in 1959.

Likewise, direct-mail associations predicted bleakly that any increase in these rates would result in a serious decline in direct-mail use. The facts show a steady and very substantial rise in volume of third-class mail throughout the decade of the 50's.

I would hasten to add at the same time that these attitudes are not representative of all publishers and direct-mail advertisers; many have shown a statesmanlike willingness to give fair consideration to this issue on its merits.

Especially has this been true of newspaper publishers, many of whom have spoken in support of Post Office requests at the rate hearings. Over 90 per cent of the editorials in the nation's newspapers during our efforts to obtain postage-rate increase have favored pay-as-you-go rates. Their publishers have been true to their responsibilities both as the voice of the public and as businessmen.

It is also true, certainly, that a great many men in business management agree that third-class postage should not in all honesty be exempted from a program to put the postal service on a sound operating basis.

This position was well expressed by Mr. Farley, who came

239

to testify at the 1956 hearings as a major executive of one of the nation's largest companies. Stating that his own company would pay whatever increased rates were necessary to erase postal deficits, he added, "I believe that all substantial business corporations in this country would feel the same way."

Later, with his own personal touch, Mr. Farley remarked, "I have always felt that the second-class mail should carry a greater load than it does now. I watch these letter carriers in New York. I walk up Park Avenue every morning and talk to these fellows. They are loaded down most of the time with magazines. I do not know what percentage of their load it is, but I would suppose that about 75 per cent of their load every day is in magazines or newspapers of some character.

"There is no reason in the world why they [the publishers] should not pay their share."

Both Mr. Farley and former Postmaster General Jesse Donaldson, either in person or by letter, have testified consistently and strongly in favor of putting the postal service on a pay-its-own way basis.

Mr. Donaldson stated in part at the 1957 hearings:

"I appeared before this committee in 1949, again in 1951, and again on April 19, 1956, in support of increased postal rates. The Congress increased rates in 1949 and again in 1951, but not to the level warranted by increased salaries for postal personnel, increased transportation costs and other costs of operating the postal service. . . .

"Postage rates are the same today as in 1932 for first-class mail and there has been only a small increase, percentage-wise, in other classes of mail. . . . There will be no decrease in the operating expenses in the years ahead; in fact, costs will increase, and it is imperative that Congress take prompt action to increase the postal rates. . . . .

"There are some who argue that the Post Office Department is a service agency, and see no need for increased postage rates. They overlook the fact that they pay in taxes for money withdrawn from the Treasury to meet deficits. . . .

"The Postmaster General has presented a good case and furnished supporting data to justify the increases proposed in the bills. Having had experience with postal deficits, I would like to see favorable action on this rate increase very early."

There *is* a durable solution to the postal budget problem.

However politely it might be phrased, the answer lies in giving the postal service the responsibility and the obligation to set its affairs in order and to operate as the basic organization it is—a business in the public service.

The present system does not properly serve the public interest.

Six months before a new fiscal year begins (the fiscal years of the Government run from each July 1 to the following June 30) the Post Office Department must try to guess the growth and demands of service in the next year and give the Congress an estimate of its costs.

The President sends these estimates along in his annual Budget Message. Thereafter, the Congress, first in its committees selected by the House and Senate and then in floor debate, conducts hearings and to a degree studies the estimates and the resultant requests for appropriations.

There is little realism in the debates. Appropriations ordinarily come close to the requests, but it is another story entirely in respect to recommendations for rates to cover the costs. It is another story, too, when Congress decides to increase the postal payroll or transportation bill beyond all recommendation of the Department without providing means of meeting the extra costs created.

Normally, requests for operating funds for the Post Office are cut a little, as some of the elected lawmakers—usually the majority party—seek to carry home the story that they helped cut government expenses.

Thus we have a situation in which the largest public service, bound by the complete dictates of the Congress, is unable either to set its own house in order or to create a break-even balance between its outlays and its income.

The crux of the matter is that the Post Office should be put in a position to run a service without profit or without loss, and then given the flexibility of management to make the adjustments of revenues and costs by which this can be done.

So far as possible, we have removed political patronage from direct influence in the postal service.

It should be possible also to abolish the politics of outside control from its operations.

What I propose is that the complicated and technical process of equitable postal-rate-making be handled by the establishment of an independent commission of rate-making authorities to be known as a "Board of Postal Rates and Fees." The members of such a commission would be appointed by the President for an indefinite term. The Board itself would be authorized to conduct investigations, hold hearings and propose adjustments in the postal-rate structure consistent with the public interest, so that postal revenues may approximately equal postal expenses.

These recommendations, after approval by the Postmaster General, would be reported by him to the Congress whenever he deemed it necessary and desirable and would take effect within ninety days from the date of presentation, providing the Congress did not within that period pass a concurrent resolution stating that it did not favor such changes.

Given reasonable attention by the Congress, this procedure, which contains adequate safeguards of all interests properly involved in the postal service, would provide the flexibility necessary if this gravely mounting problem is to be satisfactorily solved.

I believe this solution, or one like it, will come to pass. One of our great heritages as a people is our ability, when the truth is widely enough known, to accomplish seemingly impossible steps that are essential to our progress.

The accomplishment will come in this instance, I believe, when the American people become fully determined that their postal establishment should be operated on a more nearly self-supporting basis. They will then send to the Congress men and women who will see that this is done.

In concluding my story, let me re-emphasize that communications—the sum and total of our service and purpose in the postal establishment—are rapidly bringing peoples in all parts of the world more closely together. Nothing can be more important than communications to the eventual securing of that measure of understanding and trust which will promote an enduring peace.

It must be our first objective to continue building the kind of country in which, through processes of free and individual initiative, such vital developments as great communication systems are made possible.

I am confident the American people in the years ahead will go forward in freedom to an even better life than they enjoy today. I am equally confident that a healthy and vigorous United States Post Office Department can keep pace with the needs of our growing nation.

INDEX

INDEX

INDEX

Jackson, Andrew, 52
Jackson, Andrew, stamp, 115
Jackson, Nyle M., 174
Jackson, James, 42
Jefferson, Thomas, 17, 38, 39
    quote from, on American Credo stamp, 117
    stamp, 114
jet planes, mail transported by, 193
job grading, 212
job opportunities
    in postal service, 186, 187
    mail "racket" in, 159
Johansen, August E., 238
Jones, Rowland, Jr., 172
Julius Caesar's courier service, 18
juvenile delinquency. See obscenity, mail-order

Kasson, John A., 81
Kendall, Amos, 52, 53
Key, Francis Scott, quote from, on American Credo stamp, 117
Kieb, Ormonde A., 170, 174
Knight, Jack, 93, 94
Kossuth, Lajos, 121
Kuchel, Thomas H., 238

lease system, commercial-type. See buildings, post-office
Lehigh System, 196
letter carriers. See carriers, mail
letter rates, international airmail, 122
letters, number of, per year (1953), 11
Letter Writing Week, International, 82
Liberty Bell stamp, 122–23
Life Insurance, Government Group, 234
Lincoln, Abraham
    letter, 15
    postal service aided by, 75
    quote from, on American Credo stamp, 117
    stamps, 112, 115, 123
Lindquist, H. L., 119
literature, stamp, 31
lockboxes, 181

Lockwood, Richard, 120
Longacre, James B., 62
Lonely Hearts clubs, mails used by, 155, 157
    See also frauds, mail
losses, annual, postal. See deficits, postal
lottery law violated by mail, 159, 160
Louis XI of France, King. See postal service, first modern
Loveland, Governor, 29
Lubalin, Herb, 120
luxury, mail service originally a, 17, 76
Lyons, Eugene J., 172, 174, 213

McCarthy, Dr. Shane, 147
McDowell, Dr. Ephraim, stamp, 124–25
McGraw, Curtis W., 172
McKibbin, John M., 173
McLean, Evalyn Walsh, 65
McLean, John, 46
McNamara, Raymond V., 210–11
Madison, James, 17, 39
magazines
    early postal rates for, 45
    volume of, distributed by mail (1959), 25
Magsaysay, Ramon, stamp, 121
mails
    average user of the, 21
    concept of the, 17
    cost of carrying, 57
    intercity, 23, 166
    per capita, annual, 231
    volume of, daily, 176; yearly, 220, 231
    See also sanctity of the mails
mail carriers. See carriers, mail
mail-carrying trains, decline of, 193
mail contracts, relation of, to transportation, 190 ff.
Mailflo, 182–83
mailman
    first modern, 76
    pioneer flying, 93
    See also carriers, mail

250

INDEX

INDEX

post roads (*continued*)
  canals declared to be, 44
  railroads become, 44, 54
post routes
  length of, in 1795, 38; in 1800, 38
  waterways declared to be, 44
  See also routes
power, early postal service a symbol
  of, 17, 18
prepayment, compulsory for postage,
  in 1855, 63
printed cancellation, 110
printed word, low mailing rates for,
  64
privilege, early mail service a, 18
profit, 43
promotions, 217
Providence, Rhode Island, 179 ff.
"provisionals, Postmasters'," 62, 63
public information service, 212
Public Law 68, 234
public relations, stamp program allied to, 116
Puskar, Charles, 210

rackets, mails used to promote. *See*
  frauds, mail
Radio Corporation of America, 207
"railhead," 78
rail-highway services, combination,
  199, 200
"railroad post offices," 195
  abandonment of, 79
  inauguration of, 75, 78
railroads, 14, 54, 65, 77, 179, 190,
  231
  become post roads, 44, 54
  the backbone of the postal trans-
    portation system, 105
  See also transportation
railroad transportation
  decline of, due to curtailed train
    schedules, 105
  postal service support of, 192, 193
"Railvan," 200
rates, international postage, confusion
  concerning, 80
rates, postage

rates, postage (*continued*)
  comparison of early, with present-
    day, 24
  computing, 191, 242
  Congressional hearings, 239
  favored for second- and third-class
    mail, 233
  first-class mail in 1800, 17
  letter, in 1845, 54–55
  parcel post, 191, 192
  pay-as-you-go plans for, 239 ff.
  relation of, to increased costs,
    233
  triple, for express service, 54
"Red D" lines, 190
Rees, Edward H., 238
"reforms," postal service, in 1845, 55
Regional Operations Directors, 179
registered mail, 66, 79
  Hope Diamond transported by, 65
  meaning of term, 67
  safety of, 66
Regulus, the, 188, 189
regular stamps, design of, changed at
  intervals, 111
  See also design, stamp
Reorganization and Codification Act,
  Great Postal, of 1872, 138
research, postal service, 166
retirement costs, 191
Reuter stamp, 121
revenue, postal, 33, 36, 38, 53, 219ff.,
  232, 238
  in colonial days, 32, 33
  in 1815, 43
  Los Angeles post office, 178
  New York post office, 178
  surplus, under the Founding Fa-
    thers, 235
  See also deficits, financial affairs
Rizley, Ross, 171, 172
robbery of the mails, 131, 132, 134,
  135
Robert Heller & Associates, Inc., 172
Robertson, Albert J., 171, 172
Robertson, A. Willis, 238
Robey, Mr., 109
Rockwell, Norman, 119, 120
Roosevelt, Franklin D., stamps, 112

INDEX